HOME IS WHERE THE HEART IS AN ADOPTION AND BIOLOGICAL REUNION STORY

A MEMOIR

Published by No Press Yet

All Rights Reserved
Library of Congress Cataloging in Publications
1-10547804110

written by Jenni Alpert ("Cami")
excerpts by Don Logsdon

Those Experiencing or Choosing Homelessness Statistics and Solutions courtesy
of Hope of the Valley (Postscripts)

Foster Care, Adoption, & Adoption Constellation Statistics and Suggestions
courtesy of Celia Center Inc. (Epilogue)

Book formatting & layout designed by: Jose O.
Contact: joseey245@gmail.com

(*All blue text are searchable in Google for hyperlinks)

STORY

This memoir recounts a remarkable journey of the adopted self and a transformative biological reunion bound to touch your heart. Years after being taken away from her birth parents as a baby by the state and then being adopted out of the foster care system at age four, singer-songwriter Jenni Alpert decided to search for her birth father with the help of a private investigator, resumed her birth name 'Cami' to be recognized by him if reunited, and finally finds him roaming the streets of Long Beach homeless, addicted, and running from the law, yet a musician just like her. In a world where homelessness has become more prevalent today than ever, this biological duo partner up and tackle the impossible. Together they embark upon profound adventures of transformation as 'Cami' takes her birth father under her wing using unique solution solving systems to shadowing him through transitions pioneering a path to his release from the legal system for the first time since he was nine and ending his cycle of homelessness all the while motivating his halt of his drug use and street crime. Through resilience, volunteering, and sharing their story they partner together and work to inspire others experiencing homelessness, addiction, and loss along the way. While following 'Cami' discovering the roots of her adopted self and the reunification with her birth father, this dynamic story ultimately reflects the impact of how creating a common ground of togetherness despite dichotomy can spark lifelong profound transformations. As the biological duo explore their vastly contrasting worlds playing music together and giving back, they meld an incredible bond of an extraordinary partnership and unconditional love between them.

Today Jenni Alpert 'Cami' and her birth father Don continue to share their stories and songs from city to city in rescue missions, shelters, and local music venues with others facing similar challenges surrounding homelessness, addiction, incarceration, foster care, adoption, and biological reunions. Their journey continues to impact those who discover them. Look out for Homeless: the Soundtrack a short documentary that captures the early stages of 'Cami' and Don's biological reunion story which intimate documents a courageous journey nestled in the larger pressing issue of homelessness not only in Los Angeles, but all around the globe.

DEDICATION

This is dedicated to all members of my adoption constellation, all my family, and friends alike. Thank you for withstanding the foregoing of my difference and for finding a way to love me somewhere in your heart. To my mother Jill and my father Bill, my Granda Horty, my three brothers, and all my extended family. To Paul, Shelly, Amanda, Elaine, Chelsea, Chaz, Steven, Greg, Carrie, Jen, Jeff, G. U. Sol, G. A. Blanch, Uncle Jimmy, Ramon, Ramona, Steve, Jake, Joyce, G. U. Michael, Cathy, Connie, Judges and the Police, Lindsay, Mayim, Nicole, Sinem, Abby, Eric B, Damon, Justin F, Jimmy P, Chris J, Brogan, NB, John Classick, Jordy, Brian P, Mr G, Mr Kissaine, Kenny Burrell, Al Bradley, UCLA and Faculty, all my friends overseas, Jeanette, Justin C, Steve and Paula Mae, Irene, Officer B, Officer L, Laurie and Ken and Hope of the Valley, Celia Center, my birth grandparents, birth great grandparents, and the greats before that, my ancestors, my birth mother....

...and especially, to my birth father Don.

THE CONTENTS

~ PART 1 ~

Home is Where the Heart Is, An Adoption Story
Family Lines and Blood Ties

~ PART 2 ~
Home is Where the Heart Is, A Biological Reunion Story
My Birth Father and Me

"I remember the police car ride, my short legs and large black shoes dangling down the backseat, and the station piled with papers on tan colored desks with the swinging door entrance quite well - the door that opened to the rest of my life....."

PRELUDE:
THE OCTAGON IS ME

Everybody has a valuable story to tell. I was never too focused on my story per-say, that is until I chose to look for my birth father...

Everybody has a valuable story to tell. I was never too focused on my story per-say, that is until I found my birth father. Yet, I've always been comfortable and open with sharing the many different aspects and complexities that I've experienced in my life because connecting with others through raw honesty for the purpose of achieving a deeper understanding has always been a very important value to me.

When I chose to look for my biological father the summer of 2016, who at the time was a raging addict, living homeless by choice, and running from the law, one of the main motivating factors that inspired me was to figure out where I came from, to see if my birth father was still alive, and to find out who he was because I was starting to desire having a family of my own one day and he was the missing piece of my identity that Knew very little detail about except what both the court papers had revealed and what my adoptive and

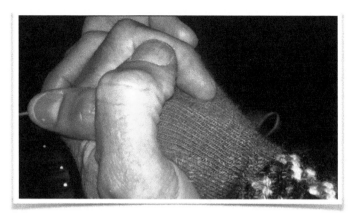

birth family members I had already found and met up to this point had told me. The missing piece about my unknown life, from having been placed in foster care upon my birth and then adopted out by the age of four after having been through four or five different homes, and even after having met some maternal birth relatives in college, wasn't filled and my curiosity began to once again nag at me. Despite what I had already learned about my adoption, there was still a lot I didn't fully know yet. Outside of court papers and assumptions or reasoning of others, I myself still always wanted to know more about my DNA lineage and where it was I came from. After so many failed relationships with hopeful beginnings, it was now time for me to fill in the holes and explore the paternal side of my life both for myself and for my future family one day.

Based on what I had compiled from all the court case documents surrounding my adoption, all the hearsay, the support from my adoptive parents whom I love very much, and care from all the other loving people in my life, I was content to leave well alone for a long time. Yet, after many failed relationships with hopeful beginnings and an urge to maybe have a family of my own one day, I finally felt ready to fill in the holes of my adopted self and set out to explore the paternal side of my lineage. So, following extensive research and reconnaissance, I finally decided to find out who my birth father really was and if in fact he was even still alive. And through the graces of possibility, the most profound journey of my life began and it was then that everything changed....

CHAPTER 1
LINEAGE, FROM THE BEGINNING

I've been wanting, for as long as I can remember, to write a memoir penning the life and journey of a fostered adopted child grown into an independent self reliant recording and touring musician who in search of a deeper sense of self goes on an adventure of a lifetime over the course of several years searching for and reuniting with birth family members to illuminate the profound value of knowing the very fabric from which you came.

Once meeting birth maternal living relatives upon my birth mother's passing before ever getting to meet her, many connections and stories would be shared. And although advised against so, in the years to follow I would ultimately research my birth father's whereabouts with the help of a private investigator and reunite with him while he was living homeless more often by choice under freeway underpasses or behind dumpsters running from the law while otherwise being regularly incarcerated for drug use and drug related crimes.

This recurring pattern would continue throughout the majority of his life partly due to his lifestyle of street life and using drugs starting at the young age of 9, and partly in survival of what life did not present him until meeting me, his daughter many years later. It was then for both of us that everything changed.

This is also when I would come to find, unbeknownst to me, that he too was a musician himself, just like me.

And further perhaps, I would continue to share in chapters the many details thereafter of our biological reunion after it first took place on the streets of Long Beach, California July 26, 2016 just shy of five years ago this coming summer. And that with the effort of research, reconnaissance, and the help of many resources gathered, my story would continue to divulge how devising creative solution solving steps for my birth father inspired and aided him in choosing to walk an uncharted path towards assimilation and integration.

Guided by present moment intuition and several past experiences that my personal life tool belt had from having volunteered for non profits prior that ranged from work with those experiencing homelessness, foster care, incarceration, and addiction coupled with my own life stories unfolding all while studying Ethnomusicology at UCLA, our miraculous path of transformation would ultimately be guided by what I would call a series of solution solving suggestions and creative encounters called family fun field trips devised intentionally combining the parallels of familiarity and otherwise newisms through adventure and discovery for my birth father to experience with me as his advocate and daily shadow, despite our dichotomous worldly exposure, which ultimately paved an unexpected journey for the both of us that unfolded into an extraordinary partnership.

This true story would detail where together with creative approaches, how he and I throughout our biological reunion journey manage to not only alter the patterns of my birth father's life of street survival and petty crime and guide him towards newly found creative transformative options for stable ground, but also would become the motivation and inspiration that lead us to work together as volunteers with our story and song to help others in similar situations see creative options for themselves as well...

but then, I would have to start at the very beginning......

CHAPTER 2
BEFORE IT ALL BEGAN

Words and a safe space to speak to a child once without a voice is like honey to bees, but I am not the very beginning. Not at all.

Don's life was preceded by the adventure of my biological great grandfather Hewitt, before he created Don's father James Royal Logsdon among the many others. Hewitt was most known for galavanting the lands any lady strolled on, making children of many fathering hardly none, following footsteps as an outlaw of sorts coupled with trying his taste at an honest living for survival. Known throughout the towns as a watchmaker to trade, he also knew music well enough to teach and conduct it, eventually making money during the depression in the 1930's as a conductor in residence for the Dallas Philharmonic Orchestra for a short while employing the likes of musicians such as Glenn Miller, Harry James, and Tommy Dorsey who also desperately were in of need work at the time. Though it was noted not much a record shows for it, nonetheless Hewitt never departed from the Texas state until his death.

As 1951 came around, the Korean War was well underway and the first son of Hewitt's James Royal Logsdon would go on to join the United States Navy. James had a mind for both engineering and music, and though not much a formal education for the former, he became a mechanic for the Navy ships as well as played self taught boogie-woogie saloon style piano upon them to entertain his Navy buddies as the war passed. But two years later he was honorably discharged due to an injury onboard a ship while working and was dropped off in Long Beach, California where he and his friend would then scour The Pike night after night for women not much different than his father before.

In 1954, James would meet and fall in love with Madonna who was escaping the

Catholic clause of her rigid upbringing at the time, happy to join in union for her escape, setting forth the next chapter of the Logsdon lineage but only now in California.

Once having several children to raise with one government military check that would regularly run low between fights in the homestead, James tried to pick up several different trades to care for the three sons he made and the three children that would later follow with other men with Madonna's search to bore a daughter. By 1968 the emotional stability of the family unit faded so drastically while the financial hardships were so plentiful, that Madonna and James welcomed in a second family of nine to share in the responsibilities of all the children and the rented two bedroom dwelling they had, creating a space filled with over eleven children and four adults on the premises at the time.

Sharing food stamps and any government income available to them still wasn't enough to manage such an unstable foundation, that ultimately, both the financial struggles and relationship incompatibilities brought more stress than the marriage could withstand. By 1969 James and Madonna would part ways but keep the marriage for legal reasons in order to somehow continue to care for the children they shared Jimmy, Michael, and their youngest Don Logsdon amongst the others that later came.

Family stories later said that my great Grandfather Hewitt Barbar Logsdon was connected to English Royalty by way of Scotland, relative somehow of Duke of the house of Windsor, and several lifetimes later upon arriving to Ellis Island continuing West settling in Tennessee and then Texas, additional mention of there being ties between his mother's side related to Daniel Boone, whilst his father's side somehow related to Davy Crockett.

Yet though everyone has history coming from somewhere and every story to tell has many perspectives point of view, the only true connection we know of to these claims for sure is the flashes of genetic DNA memory my birth father and I would later discover that we both separately share before being told directly by anyone in our shared family line and before having formally met one another until in adulthood ourselves - a familiarity of all those such past times mentioned merely documented by family folktales handed down, but that will be for another chapter.

May the tides between truth and tales be the blood that binds us.

CHAPTER 3
MY BIRTH FATHER DON'S EARLY CHILDHOOD

"The first thing that happened was when I was about seven years old is I didn't like how I felt and was on the search for anything that would improve the way I felt. By age five I found a cigarette in the alley and a box of matches and smoked tobacco for the first time, and it was on." (Excerpt by D. Logsdon)

By age nine was the first time I smoked a joint. In them days you would purchase a cigarette for a quarter. I found a half of a joint on the street, headed for the bushes, and smoked that until it was gone and that was the second sign I found that improved the way I felt.

After that I came about finding reds and whites; benzedrine, dexedrine, methedrine - uppers and downers, pills and decided to try those. By age ten I checked out any liquor they had at any store I could steal from, red ripple wine and tequila were my favorites.

The neighborhood we lived in was just that, a row of duplexes and apartments with a few small houses here and there. From the outside, ours was a two bedroom duplex that we lived in but on the inside cluttered and crowded was our sense of home. The layout had a den between the kitchen and the living room next two the two small bedrooms where all areas would be blocked off for more rooms, even the kitchen, for friends and other people, or other kids there, maybe fifteen or twenty Bell Gardens white boys would be around there around the clock living in every square inch of the house all the time which was good news as far as I was concerned giving me an advantage towards how to live like an adult, though by then I was only twelve.

The room I would stay in there had a bunk bed for me and my two other brothers and some of the neighborhood kids who needed places to sleep. I would make most of the meals myself for the rest of family and people there because I seemed good at making the eggs and my mom was a homebody lady who spent most of her time as an overseer for the several families and kids all around the neighborhood that were crammed inside our home so I helped when I could.

From the earliest I could remember there were cockroaches, rats, and trash piling to the ceiling while outside my dad and his friend tried to work on several automobiles at once in our driveway for a time to make money, so see, there was not room for much but it didn't really bother me any. There would be green trash dumpsters down the alley where my brothers and I would take the trash out when we weren't smoking and playing cards out back. Pretty soon this would become my main chore along with cooking for the lot of the mouths on the premises, and managing the numerous cats and rodents that hung around. I once even saved a little duck. He was my special friend until the cockroaches got too much and when I tried to get them gone by spraying them with raid, I lost my favorite duck friend too. That was real sad. I didn't use raid anymore. As for rats, yeah the whole house was full of them, but I didn't mind, I felt like I was raising them anyway.

Once my mom invited a second whole family to live with us to share in our small space and the financial responsibility, this would be the first experience I had with architecture and design when I found myself dividing up the small space splitting each rooms into twos or threes with sheets and blankets for walls so for everyone could fit inside. If I could of finished school outside of later getting a GED during one of my times in prison, I know next to being a guitar player, I would of been an architect. I always loved looking at those New York and Chicago Buildings in the books they had in their libraries. Building those would be something.

Throughout the day around the clock, and believe me I didn't care what time it was, in order for me and my brothers to get food and money and drugs we would go around and about stealing whatever we could find and swiping pop bottles that back then were of value to trade in for cash. Once a week we'd have our big hit when a swap-meet would open where we could steal bicycles to sell for more money to live on. Another thing we would do is find newspaper dispenser machines that at the time cost a quarter for a newspaper and we would stick bubble gum on the on a popsicle stick then slide it between the metal plate so it could get at the quarter other people previously spent to buy their paper. It was kind of like slot gambling and pretty fun actually.

My oldest brother Jimmy, and two closest friends at the time Earl Simmons and Butchy Williams started a crew with some of the other neighborhood boys and banned together for survival. Though I was only ten at the time, the youngest member, I was proud to be part of the gang and proud to call them family for their protection and guidance to prosper together. Stealing became our means to gain stability out of the otherwise poverty we were born into. The money ultimately was used to buy as many drugs and alcohol bottles as we could get which became my favorite pastime to escape to.

You gotta realize, I lived around and about twenty five to thirty adults when I was ten to twelve years old and every one of them were drunks, drug addicts, pool players, rode motorcycles, bet on horses, and were gamblers. They were the normal people that I would know of since day one. To me following in their footsteps and joining them in drinking, drugs, gambling, and adventures was exactly the thing to do.

Even from the early age of 9, I found school to be a complete waste of time and completely boring so I would ditch and head to the railroad tracks to drink red ripple wine and try the reds and whites I had bought with my older brothers. The adventure of stealing and ditching were not only exciting to me but moreover a means to an end and an escape from the otherwise dull or overcrowded world I knew.

■ ■

As I started to ditch more and increase my drug interest, by now at age 11, I got caught by the truancy officer at my elementary school when he followed me skipping school through the alley where he saw me steal a basket of pop bottles. He came to me at my house with the Bell Gardens police, pushed into my room and saw liquor bottles and trash all over the floor, which lead to the search in my pockets where they found an enormous amount of drugs and said to me for the first time but definitely not for the last, "you are being placed under arrest."

There were three charges. The first: possession of drugs - marijuana, Seconal, and Benzedrine, the second: possession of stolen property due to the stolen bicycle I had in my room along with the two shopping carts of pop bottles there that they knew I had stolen from down the alley earlier that day, which is how they caught me following me home, and the third charge: truancy, having ditched school seven times, two over there limit getting me ten hard swats on the ass with a wooden paddle by the principal, which for me by now was an all to regular past time at school to begin with, and then they kicked me out of school for the rest of the semester which I wasn't bothered at all by, but what I didn't release was, instead, I was being taken to Juvenile Hall for my first of many more times to come.

With my parents growing disdain for one another and deep struggle for money and food, their arguing pursued as a regular pastime between them. It was anything we could do outdoors to enjoy life the way we wanted to. It was also during this period that I started going in and out of foster homes and juvenile halls regularly for the correctional efforts the city authorities tried to instill to no avail. For my older brothers being in and out of group homes, juvenile halls, and work camps was they same for them as well and for all the same reasons but the counselors would bring them to visit me in the TMV unit in Central Juvenile Hall to visit me where I was so I always had a sense of family near.

Though my mother had her ups and downs, she always for my whole life would do her best to support me the ways she knew how, sending me packages when I needed them, and by twelve years of age, bringing me both a guitar and a chess set to learn in one of the four Juvenile Halls I was moved around in to help me pass the time. Once I had a guitar and the game of chess to play, the other kids wouldn't beat me up as much. I struggled with being locked in our rooms throughout the nights without access to the hallway bathrooms and would still get into trouble for wetting the bed, but I always had my guitar and I always had the past grandmasters of chess to play games from the books that kept me company, taught me the game with the books written about them, and safe from the outside world.

It was also during these years when I would be released either for good behavior or for time served starting at about age eleven, that I would find for the first time what it was like to make out with girls. I was a little young kid who knew damn well what it was like to lay around with naked ladies alright. Any age, my brothers would set it up or they would come find me in my chosen hiding places. This would also set the stage for the later years in my life with the many women I would come to know briefly while my main love most often later would become heroin herself."

It was also around this time, that my birth father Don's parents argued day and night about anything and everything, money, instability, space, among the several other issues, they simply started to fall out and so she started to mess around with a new man. Both the financial hardships their marriage was to create and the lack of connection between them put his father, my paternal birth grandfather, into such a mental rage that he would check himself into Metro Mental Hospital for the first time that summer, but it would hardly be the last. Throughout the next twenty plus years don's father never quite came back from his mental breakdown and the red crisis squad car would become a frequent means of transportation  to and from the mental hospital, the first trip also being the one that would set forth the motion of his next relationship upon meeting my soon to become birth mother, Mary-Lou Morantz.

CHAPTER 4

MY BIRTH MOTHER MARY LOU THE FINE ARTIST, AND FROM WHERE SHE CAME

All the way across town on the 'finer' side of life lived a young pretty woman with high desires to become an interior designer. Her name was Mary Lou. With fine art as her main medium she had an eye for style.

Having just gotten into UCLA herself, one of the most renowned schools for its kind she was excited to expand her horizons for the finer things in life. She had even already garnered an opportunity to help a new budding hair stylist in the Melrose area not far from where she grew up in Beverly Will in proper upper middle class Conservative Jewish household. She got attention for being the first interior decorator to paint the hair salon all black which set in motion a high visible business for the then budding salon owner. Everyone in town knew of his salon from then on.

My birth mother Mary Lou's paternal grandparents, having migrated first from Denver then to Canada and finally settling in Los Angeles one after another confirmed to have been part of bringing the first Kosher Meat Packing business to downtown LA joining Abe's brother Sam, making a huge stamp on the Los Angeles Jewish scene at one time. Also having aiding in the building and development of

a small conservative Jewish Temple on Olympic Boulevard, it was said that the Jewish community valued the Morantz family for more than one reason.

For the voice she has not, let my heart speak.

■ ■

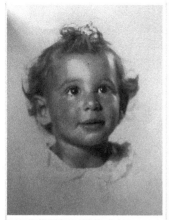

My birth mother to be, Mary Lou herself was no stranger to debutant life. She was even part of the National Charity League Los Angeles Chapter with her mother as a teen volunteering to help those in need. Coincidentally, I was too, unbeknownst to this knowledge in my teen life, a member of the NCL San Fernando Chapter to volunteer and help people with my mom who adopted me, but perhaps it wasn't so coincidental at all.

I was also told later that it was in fact my birth grandfather Lou Lou who was to step in during my foster care situations whilst a court case was dragging on to decipher who in what family may get and keep me, and it was his final push and demand that I be released and put up for adoption by a like minded stable Jewish family somewhere far enough away to keep me safe, yet close enough to my roots for my name.

Mary Lou would often would hear the stories told by her father of her grandparents, my great grandparents Abe and Celia self identified as zionists in hopes of aiding the Jewish

people to have a homeland, making huge efforts to be part of helping Israel become free state just after World War II, even obtaining land there. The history goes even further than that on both maternal great great sides was a lineage line all the way to Odessa, Russia and Latvia before the wagon days in the US.

As it were, and still is in many ways today, the commitment to culture, heritage, and tradition was embedded strong for as far back as anyone in the family could remember. Tradition lives on in those who carry it.

My birth maternal grandfather Lou Lou was born with an older brother and two younger sisters making for quite a large extended family to come. While my birth maternal grandmother Geraldine had a sister and a brother who stayed behind in Denver, she herself came to Los Angeles for something new, reacquainted with Lou Lou from childhood in Denver when she arrived here, and hence the next chapter started.

But as in Jewish custom where it is the way of the culture and community to pass down the stories and laws, the many generations akin back then passed down their conservatism as well, so as the temperament and often control.

Elite card games would take place weekly with fine wines and cognac in their fancy homes of Beverly Will that the life and heritage before now afforded them. My maternal grandparents Lou Lou and Geri inviting all Lou's siblings now married and close by in walking range to enjoy the weeks hard earned dollar by the fine dining and card games they chose, the children often locked away in the back rooms with loneliness and resentment as their playmates while the adults enjoyed their luxury and parties. Love would feel lost at times, though not always. It just was what it was.

As the Kosher Meat Packing business began to fail, gambling a hefty dime came to be the regular past time, the stress on the families to keep the class going took its toll just the same as any other family might face, but manifested itself in the fabric of the family foundations in slightly different ways.

Businesses ended, separations were made, divorces were settled, and children fell to the mercy of circumstance, but class still remained even if merely a shadow of apparition to give a stable impression to all. It was said my birth uncle, younger brother to my birth mother, felt the hardest bruises from the fall, in and out of Vista Del Mar Children's Group Home himself before later taking up road management life for the band Spirit and key marijuana sales man during the time when it was still very illegal. But his charm was his greatest asset and did him well nonetheless.

■■

Geri, my birth grandmother, was said to be an adventurous woman, known for her love of convertible Cadillacs, Jackie O Hare sunglasses, and her hair up in a bonnet. It was even mentioned that she raced down the PCH highway in Malibu one Sunday with kids in the car to catch the sunset of freedom.

Stormy at home, all the children alike could feel the thunder coming. It was much easier to keep busy and in Mary Lou's, case being the oldest female of them all, keeping pretty, pruned, and creative mainly as a painter in her spare time would work for a while.

It didn't take long however, for trips to San Francisco to go underway during the early sixties which set her on another path unexpectedly for Miss Mary Lou. There are several stories of explanation for what horror for the family related to her was to happen next. Some say she was a to young a woman in San Francisco with a then boyfriend and took too much acid by accident while experimenting. Others suggest she actually suffered a major traumatic event by several men she knew while being dosed against her knowledge or will. No reason is clear for why she lost her mind and entered the depths of a hybrid state of catatonic schizophrenia coupled with raging episodes of delusional madness that was scary enough for anyone to see, especially those closest to her that lost her as she slipped away into another realm never to completely come back from. Family secrets are meant to be respected. The shame of it all simply was too much to bear.

Immediately it became clear that Metropolitan Mental Hospital, the best known of its kind back then, would be the place for her to be sent away to, if not to try to manage what now was, at least to protect the family name.

Metropolitan Mental Hospital was a scary place though where shock therapy and sedation were the norm. It is said that she never was to paint again after being admitted there. But with a conservator now at her aid, and a ward of the state managed by someone, it wasn't much of a surprise that her beauty still managed to attract a young gentleman a few years her senior who at that very same time had admitted himself there due to a failing marriage and to the many overwhelming financial stresses that went with it, none other than a man named ....

James Royal Logsdon.

CHAPTER 5
I AM MY OWN COUNTRY

For people who have relationships with their blood family it's a given and a gift that they get to see who they look like, what traits, characteristics, and talents they may have inherited. But as someone who was in foster care....

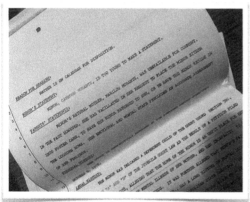

When I was a little girl just about five years old while seated in my new grandma's kitchen, pencil and paper in hand by request finally adopted into what would become my forever home, my Grandma Horty watching me intently told me I was gonna be a writer one day. Thank you Grandma for never making me feel less than capable and always ensuring that I had some sense of self confidence when I really needed some. Maybe you were right....

For people who have relationships with their blood family, it's a given – and a gift that they get to see who they look like, who they sound like, and what traits, characteristics, and talents they may have inherited. But as someone who was in foster care from my birth until I was 3 ½, I never knew. Did I look like my biological parents? Did we have similar talents and skills? Do I sound like them? I didn't have any answers, only my intuition, my instinct, and a drive to succeed and survive. Despite not knowing who my biological parents were, I knew enough to know it was a blessing that I was alive. I always felt that when we are born it's because we were lucky enough to be selected to make it here in the first place no matter where we come from or how we get here. The point being to leave behind a legacy and to contribute somehow to making the world better when we leave it than what it was when we came. It also seemed to me that a name is simply a way that others know themselves in relationship to you.

This is why I never minded that I have so many names; Cameron my intended birth name, Cami for short, Jennifer my fostered given name Jen for short, and Jenni Alpert my final adopted name once I landed my forever family home and what I ended up choosing to use as I became the budding performing singer songwriter I was to be. Just as names go, they are also titles with which to identify by; mother, sister, father, friend, a way of identifying who people are to us, and who we are to them. But what is to happen when you find you have two families somehow, maybe three or maybe even four? I find it most valuable to express why I refer to Don, for example, as my "birth father." It is to honor his role in having "invented" me, for how special a person he is in my life now which we will get too later, and most of all for him having given me life. Simultaneously, I refer to Bill Alpert who adopted and raised me until the time he passed away as my "dad" or "father" not only because of what he did to help me in my life when he was with us and for the fact that he was all I knew as a father figure through my adoption, but also because his spirit continues to support me in my life through my mom even now and I feel it is right to honor both men semantically speaking for exactly who they are. It's also important that I note before proceeding on that I do not harbor any judgment about the way people live or resentment for all that unfolded as I describe, for to me, sometimes it's not about what we have around us that matters, rather who and the understanding of it all that makes all the difference.

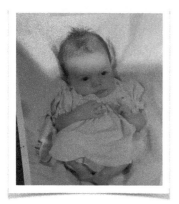 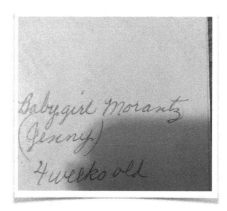

My parents Jill and Bill never met my birth parents throughout my adoption either though they knew some of the background that came with me when I first arrived at their home at age 3 1/2 before they were to become my forever parents when I was to turn 4.

I was told that I was introduced to a piano while in my second foster home and that music was always an innate interest of mine in one way or another even at an extremely young age. Upon

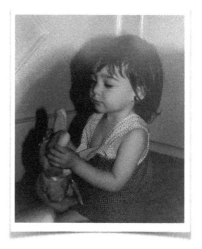

being adopted by the Alpert's, it was fortunate that they had an upright piano in their home as well and made sure to get me a pedal box fitted to my height in order for me to be able to play piano with the sustain pedal, something I loved to do often. Second to piano lessons came voice and third to that came acting classes after failing violin and flailing through dance. Finally came the guitar and then the push for further education. Later in life was when I realized how truly lucky I had been for all the opportunities I was granted to explore for my life could have been very different.

■■

Early life. The day I was born, the court system intervened for my safety due to the many details of how I came to be in this world and placed me into the first of what would be four foster homes that I rotated through until I was 3 1/2. During my time in foster care, the police would come to discover some of the dangers I was being exposed to in one foster home I had been give to unbeknownst to the state due to a tip by a bank worker who called in after an interaction she had with the lady who had come with me in her arms demanding they give a loan to her then husband and her or she couldn't be responsible for what would happen to me.

With the help of the bank the police removed me immediately, and placed me into an emergency holding group transitional group home until I became eligible for permanency with adoption.

I remember the police car ride, my short legs and large black shoes dangling down the backseat, and the station piled with papers on tan colored desks with the swinging door entrance quite well. I felt sorry for the lady and that's about the extent of my memory there.

Many years later she would find me online and show up at one of my gigs to apologize. I recognized her voice immediately while I was there alone with the sound man soundchecking for my music set. I replied a soft hello with no hard feelings to harbor as I felt her need for forgiveness lingering, but for me all that I could see was simply a woman who had tried her best with what she'd been given. I hugged her ok before strolling away to sing my song *Heaven* on stage.

Shortly thereafter, in what would start out as my fourth 'emergency' placement, the Alpert's were called and told that there was a girl available but that they had to come and get me tomorrow. So the following day, with a little bunny in hand for me, we met with my brown paper bag full of my few things, and by a specific request of my birth mother's family later I was told, I was then taken to a stable Jewish home as the rest of my life would unfold. That foster home put up a fight to keep me themselves, and though they would lose, a second court case would begin with regard to my life before I was even four.

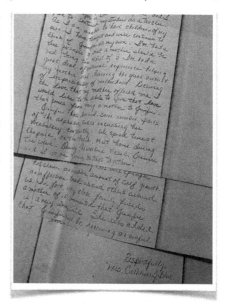

From the moment I arrived at the Alpert's, the survival skills I had gained in foster homes, namely charm and the ability to play music, helped me through the transition. My new home came with three older brothers, two of whom where my adoptive dad's birth sons who frequented our home, and the third who had been adopted also but as a baby by my mom and her previous marriage whom now lived in the same home as I did for the years before he left for college.

At 4, I was old enough to understand that I had been in foster homes; and in the process of being adopted, I had been told bits and pieces of my biological parents' story, but most of the details were kept from me until I was a teenager. Looking back on my childhood, I don't recall identifying too strongly with negativity or a sense of sadness; I was an optimistic child but I did often feel a sense of disconnection linger from time to time.

I always had an interest in my biological roots, but I was strongly advised to focus on my current life rather than to delve into any past. My adoptive parents, siblings, and extended family made sure that I understood that I was loved and wanted. They gave me the support to discover my tools and talents as well as the life skills for self-reliance of which I am forever grateful for. When I was adopted, I couldn't yet read, write, or identify letters, colors, and numbers, so my adoptive parents hired tutors to help me with my education. They fostered my love for music, composition, singing, writing songs, acting, and movement by enrolling me in various classes to help further develop my talents. They also protected me when past haunts from foster care found me and started following me to elementary school while also taking up work with my dad's good friend to try to stay close to me somehow. It was for this reason I switched schools mid year to a totally new world with new challenges to face with the harsh kids there at school.

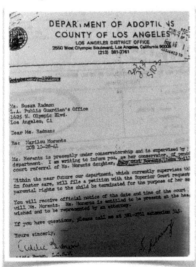 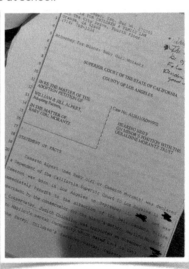

Still my artistic drive consumed a lot of my focus and my mind in healthy and positive ways throughout my childhood. From time to time in my youth, I can recall feeling emptiness: wondering exactly where it was that I came from and what my biological lineage and cultural heritage was. I often wondered if my artistic skills were genetic since none of my adoptive family was musical at all, but I was also aware that this was something I might not ever get to know.

I always knew from the moment I arrived to the Alpert's that that the people were raising me weren't the people who brought me into this world, but it was around age 11 due to a lot of contention at home as mothers and daughters often have discord from differences, is when I started to really wonder where it was that I came from. I discovered an old photo album that had traveled with me through the foster care system and while flipping through them one day, a photo fell out and happened to have notes written on the back of it notating what I guessed might of been my original last name *Morantz* so I looked up every number in the white pages and called them all to see if I could find one related to me. It wouldn't be until years later when I actually did start to meet the remaining living members of the

Morantz tree prior to my biological reunion with my birth father several years following that, but notating and researching developed among some of my many tools at a very early age.

■■

Music and me. Because I struggled with some aspects of traditional learning in school, I had planned to go to New York to live the life of a performer upon completing high school, but thanks to my adoptive parents urging, I attended UCLA and was granted a small

scholarship to entice me with their prestigious new Jazz program. While working on my degree, I began to write, record, and produce my own music alongside learning jazz.

And following, in my 20s I discovered ways to market, brand, and sell my music, tenaciously googling to connect throughout the years then recording with some the greatest producers, engineers, and musicians that I personally admired, namely; Niko Bolas, George Massenburg, Nathaniel Kunkel, Steve Greenberg, Steve Greenwell, Mikal Blue, JJ Blair, Stevie Blacke, David Pearlman, Nicola Fantazzi, Rob Matson, Doug Sax, Eric Boulanger, Russ Kunkel, Dean Parks, Matt Rollings, Viktor Krause, Jimmy Messer, Joel Martin, Jimmy Paxson, Chris Chaney, Zac Rae, and Guthrie Trapp to name a memorable few, performing all over Los Angeles, the country, and ultimately in over 14 countries around the world, with a backpack full of my CDs, my guitar

and sometimes a mini keyboard, charm, and networking skills to maintain friends and contacts in each given city in order to return again and again with their help, building before facebook existed a loyal fan base for my music while managing it all single handedly. It never much bothered me that nobody knew who I was.

Though while in foster care I experienced my first piano, it was actually in high school when I began to love to perform and speak in front of audiences in order to connect.

From being president of and a soloist in my high school choir, to becoming a proactive member of our school debate team, to joining the Model United Nations club, to being the school mascot, to set designing and acting, often staring in the school plays and musical, all my teachers along with my parents helped shaped me.

And eventually I took up songwriting on both the piano and acoustic guitar inspired by my mom's suggestion to learn to play something portable and had my heart set on heading to New York City upon graduation.

My mother on the other hand had other plans for me.

My dad Bill. It was during my junior year of high school when my father got sick with cancer. He was home with treatments a lot. Many days and nights it was just me, my mom, my dad, and the big scary c at home after school. I didn't know exactly what cancer even was as the time, but the doctor and hospital visits, millions of pamphlets, and regular treatments of all kind told me it wasn't something anyone would ever want to go through alone if they didn't have to.

All the while caring for my father, my mother was desperate for me to obtain a well rounded education despite my commitment to the arts so it was she who marked off UCLA in

my college application for the UC schools as an option because back then you could write one series of essays but apply to as many UCs as you wanted by marking off each school on the checklist.

UCLA Daze. Personally, I never really thought of college, and furthermore never even considered that I would end up going UCLA let alone get in, nor had I ever dreamed that I would even take an audition there. The day I arrived and began singing for the faculty, a man in the audience, later known as Al Bradley the admittance counselor of the department at the time, actually left mid way during my first song solidifying, for certain in my mind that I was not going to get in there. "*If I had known this was going to be a classical audition rather than performance Jazz, I would have learned an aria*" I said jokingly before my final song, put a smile on my face, persevered

on, and sang my heart out with 'Teach Me Tonight' by Sammy Cahn.

As I proceeded to swiftly walk out of the audition I was stopped for a chat by Al just outside the classical music audition room who confirmed to me that my style wasn't really a fit, which it hardly ever was anywhere anyway so I wasn't surprised, but then after a pause as I nodded and got up to leave, he took my hand and asked if I would come back and audition for the great Jazz guitarist Kenny Burrell for his new Jazz program instead later that week. *"Who?" I wondered to myself?* For at the time I knew very little about music, most only about the performance of it. But sure, what was one more drive over the hill to the city in order to miss another day of class back home to get to sing some more for whoever he was, why not.

Getting into UCLA 's Ethnomusicology Department's World Music Studies emphasis on Jazz Program coined as the first Jazz Vocalist to be admitted into the newly designed four year program was really wild to me. Though kind of par for the course in my pave it yourself kind of style, secretly, not only did I not yet know who Charlie Parker was, I really didn't even know how to read or write music much at all. This seemed a funny feat - actually getting into UCLA, but not so outlandish after all, as the rest of my independent music career and other performing ventures would unfold in similar fashion throughout the years to come. To call UCLA directly before the acceptance letters even printed just to learn the outcome so one could plan their future was equally unheard of, but when Al Bradly answered my call and replied replied *"we don't normally do this as we are not allowed to say anything until the acceptance letters are sent out, but how would you feel about being the first Jazz vocalist to enter our new four year program here at UCLA this fall?"* was a pretty amazing experience deemed accomplishment considering I had a long road ahead of me in learning how to write essays let alone a music score.

But ultimately attending UCLA made the most sense due to the fact that my father was still struggling in his third year with malignant melanoma, a cancer, rarely if ever survived. And after eleven surgeries and treatments he had throughout my senior year of high school, which seemed unbelievably unfair to all those who knew and loved him, ultimately, he left us with loving memories and a legacy of lessons for all of us to remember him by as the years would pass on without him.

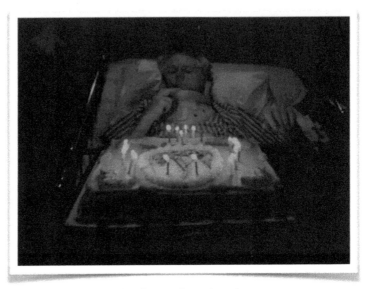

He would die my freshman year of college, a huge loss for everyone.

■■

The losses of many. My freshman year of college proved to be a collection of equal gains and losses, but the death of my birth mother never getting to meet her and just before my dad's death was another loss added to the list. I was to learn just months before losing him, that my birth mother of whom I would now never know, was to die on the sidewalk from heart failure due to a cocaine (in crack form) overdose, something she got into just after my adoption took place and never again was to kick until the end of her life.

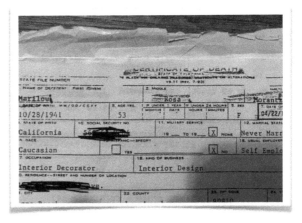

I was just 17 when my adoptive parents were informed by the state that my biological mother, Mary Lou, had died. Since at the time my adoptive father was quite ill himself, my adoptive mother waited until I was 18 to tell me, hoping I would be emotionally able to handle this information and its consequences. When Mary Lou died, I learned that my biological parents had not been in anything resembling a traditional relationship.

My biological mother conceived me in her 30s while my biological father was just 16: they were surrounded by a life of drugs and crime, and they both struggled with relationships to mental health, what I call the mental wellness spectrum. Both of them were wards of the state, my birth mother for her mental wellness challenges and my birth father for his lifestyle of drugs and petty crime thus neither one of them could be my raising parents.

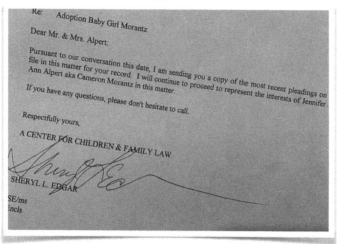

Upon her death was yet a third court case wrapped around my life; the first being my adoption case, the second being between a foster home and my now parents, and this the third which focused on a new law for adoptees to allow birth children to receive an inheritance delegated to them by birth family estates despite the separation of adoption if written into an estate plan, which is exactly what my birth grandmother, when my birth mother was to pass after her, had done for me. Apparently the two lawyers that paired up from Denver and Los Angeles were quite a team because they not only won my rights for me, but also rights for other future adoptees to come.

The biological quilt that weaves. Just after Mary Lou died, I was privileged to meet many of my biological mother's side of the family and they have been good to me ever since. I always felt so fortunate to connect with parts of my maternal side, which has deeply enriched and fulfilled a part of me. And though hearing from most everyone to never delve into the paternal side had made me honor that for most of my life, for I understood them, and loved them for their awareness and honesty, the time had come however, one day much later, for me to make a personal choice for myself, and so alone to learn of my birth paternal side, eventually I did just that.

But several years prior to the reunion story with my birth father, came the story of my birth mother though she was no longer here to tell it, and I met my maternal birth aunt, her sister first. After all, it was due to her generosity and honesty that reconnected me with the family and the family estate all together and I appreciated her and the opportunity to learn about her. Though it had been the will of my birth grandmother and my birth mother that I be written in as a bloodline member, it was my birth aunt who saw it through upon my birth mother's death and that she cared so much about my well being touched me deeply. She wasn't able to adopt me when I was little for her own reasons, so years later, when she thought of my best interest in the next best way she could, I was forever thankful for her. That small inheritance not only helped me create and release music and tour independently for quite some time, it also afforded me the creativity to interior decorate my first home which later I would share with my birth father upon reuniting with him while guiding him towards a new life in transformation. The irony of the combined support from my adoptive and birth families for my stability and well being to then lend me the foundation to help someone else was truly profound.

Prior to my first encounter with a biological relative, I consciously made an effort to ensure my birth aunt of my stability and life experience after having learned more detail of my birth mother and the dynamics that surrounded her in the court documents I received upon her death. In hopes of establishing a deep new connection I started to share myself with her by writing letters. Though she had already moved at the time from the address typed in the court papers that I had, my letter somehow ended up at her new address anyway and set forth a whole reunion story

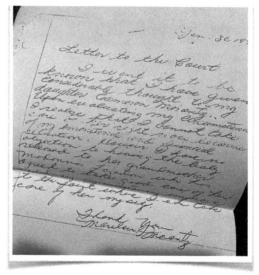

of its own though it was slightly short lived. Our first trip in person was amazing. We connected on so many things all the way to having the same perfume and taste in teas but despite all the holes she filled in for me about my birth mother and our our family tree showing me her fine art and telling me stories, I could sense her uneasiness for all the rest that began to surface which was meant to stay safely stowed away, hopefully forever. And, ultimately, and common for some biological reunions, it was too hard for her to continue to know me for all that I reminded her of. It took me many years, but eventually, I came to understand, I reminded her too much of my birth mother and of where my birth father came from, and sometimes the pain of the past is just too much for the present.

■ ■

Blood driven. My first deep long term connection with a blood relative since my birth mother's passing was with my second birth cousin Paul. He was the son of my birth grandfather's sister and a quintessential Morantz. There aren't enough pages to describe the connection we have but he did tell me more than once he didn't know whether to love me or hate me for having saved his life. At the time we

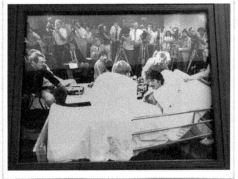

were introduced, Paul was struggling with a rare form of red blood cell aplasia that had stemmed from a cancer treatment that took away his particular cancer at the time, but left him with a list of other ailments to manage along with the depths of his mind for the rest of his life.

A survivor of a rattlesnake bite placed in his mailbox by the cult Synanon that he single handedly dismantled, left him with post traumatic haunts throughout the rest of his days. Between that and the overwhelming desire to pen his life stories and feats, for he had a lot to say and an even deeper need to be loved, he was still often met with disappointments, and that too would weigh heavily. But he inspired me so much and all I could do was admire his mind for the law and language it bared, for his stories and charisma, and his ability to follow duty as a lawyer and realize his dream as a writer, persevering with pride and passion alone.

The first weekend we spent together upon our introduction, the reunion of sorts set up by my birth Aunt for us all to meet was electric and exciting. Through her I met the most amazing birth relatives. My cousin Amanda and second cousin Shelly are extremely dear to my soul for the many memories we've shared, the sisters I never had but always wanted.

So many to mention, so many to love ... Chaz, Steven and Greg, Jen and Jeff and so many more. Each and every one a notch in my heart and a huge piece of life I love so dearly; I love you more.

What they each added made me more whole and more full. As it came to a close and everyone dispersed back to their lives when I left his home an initiative uneasy feeling lingered inside.

Later that night I impulsively drove back to find no one coming to the locked front door though the lights were on and fortunately a window open, for when I glanced inside, I saw pale Paul laying on the floor with blood escaping his nose and mouth in a pool by his face. This was the one and only time I ever had the confidence to break and enter by crawling through that window that night and I'm glad because that return afforded me many more years watching movies, listening to stories, making meals for, and spending time with with a man I was fortunate enough to know and would come to unconditionally love no matter what as an extended bloodline of my own, someone who was a sense of family, and a sense of home.

■■

I am my own country. By this time in my mid twenties, my main focus was on performing, recording, and making music which had become a daily pastime.

I'd always worn hats and had many to rotate from for myself and to get my message in music out there in the world whether it was acting as artist manager, booking agent, publicist, promoter, tour manager, record producer, songwriter or artist ... you name it, I did it for myself, paving my own way thanks to Donald Passman's book "*All You Need to Know About the Music Business*" and the pioneer of independent female musicians who I admired most at the time for the path that she paved, none other than AniDiFranco.

My simple misunderstanding that she 'did it all on her own' had me playing every role Passman outlined and defined until I myself was developing professional recordings, booking my own tours both nationally and internationally, setting up the routes to get there and back, and running the promotion for them to boot literally all by myself. In the early days while pounding the pavement playing what was called *the circuit* on little indie tours to get my music out there, I'd hub out of New York annually even though I lived in LA, my first gig ever there at The Bitter End opening for a rock singer Watt White who's leather pants split wide open mid show, "welcome to New York City bare bottoms up", as he rocked it anyway like a champ, one of the greatest performing singer - writers I first met. I'd spend my days researching artists' posters to find all the music nights, open mics, and songwriter festivals that were happening back then and would jump on the Chinatown bus north or south singing through my Taylor guitar frequenting Club Passim and the Burren in Boston, The Bitter End, CBGB's, and Sidewalk Cafe on Avenue A in Manhattan, The Point just outside of

Philly and the World Cafe, traveling onward south to Baltimore performing for the locals there before expanding to the Carolinas, Atlanta, Alabama, Nashville, then up to Detroit, Chicago singing with American Babies, then touring with Bump, opening for Kaki King, and becoming a tweener opening second sets for jam bands like Kernel Bruce Hampton and Moonshine Stills thanks to Seth and his promotion company Shimon Presents, opening for Jennifer Nettles at Eddies Attic after winning their songwriting competition one year, and supporting local touring acts in Atlanta because of Mike over at Smith's Old Bar after having already had some brief history opening for Left Over Salmon back on the West Coast by chance.

I met so many supportive and amazing people and musicians on the circuit back then, and one of the first was Hugh McGowan, a songwriter in Somerville, Ma who started and ran a music night, a staple circuit stop, at a pub called The Burren and would be one of the first to give me a chance on a big stage. It would take some time for it to hit me how sad I would become when he was to suddenly pass many years later despite our keeping in touch, for never having said exactly how much the small moments in our music friendship over the years that we shared actually surmounted to so much. And I didn't realize how much he would be missed and how much I had forgotten about my first few years on the road and how much those early years shaped me to be the musician I was today until he was gone. Moments in our music friendship over the years that we shared actually surmounted to so much. And I didn't realize how much he would be missed and how much I had forgotten about my first few years on the road and how much those early years shaped me to be the musician I was today until he was gone.

As the minutes dragged on from receiving the news of that great loss, moments of memories from the early days of my music adventures began to surface with reminders of the first generation of those that really helped and supported me out there. Hugh made room for me at the Burren when I showed up year after year, having me play my songs and piano with his and then opened up his home to me without fail come rain, shine, or snow - every. single. time. He became my first road music mentor and why I made sure to drive to Boston from New York to explore Boston's music city as my guide, showing me the ropes and took me around, lending me his car, and showing me how he got his music sound. *"Hugh had fostered a wonderfully inclusive environment for performing and*

listening to live music (in Somerville, MA, but really for musicians to connect somewhere musically in the US). All were welcome. You could witness somebody perform in front of an audience for the very first time, and get your mind blown by a veteran troubadour that just happened to stop by - all in the same night. It was a space to hone your craft, or just simply share in the experience over a few pints. The stage was sacred. Hugh made sure of it. Of the opportunities and community that Hugh created, it's impossible to quantify the "ripple effect" for everybody else." (Jesse D, songwriter Ma).

Despite struggling with deep dark addiction for most of his life, he was the light on the stage. Having started and ran one of the longest lasting music nights in the US of its kind, helping so many, upon Hugh's passing it really became the end of an era. He was the kind of guy who would jump in the car and come back to New York with me and my friends to perform his songs on a gig of mine just to be along for the ride, and even made sure to be in the audience years later when I graduated to touring opening act supporting Loudon Wainwright and then Luka Bloom, always treating me like a solid musician even when I was still learning and made me feel like I was somebody worth stopping for to meet and listen to.

What a privilege it is to hold such history with someone for over twenty years, and knowing me that's no small feat. Most of all his loss to addiction woke me up to remember too always to stop and call friends and family to let them know how much they mean while making sure to cherish every minute in the moments that you have together.

Hugh one was among an early select few that were a huge part of the start of my journey as a young musician along with Ken and Paul from The Bitter End and my best friend B in New York, Matt Smith from Club Passim, Jesse Lundy from The Point and Ralph in Philly, Jim in Baltimore, and Seth out in

Atlanta who put me on festivals and shows with local musicians there to name a few of them, significantly helping me develop when I first started out on the road.

Inspired by my friends, I even attempted being a promoter sometimes with small venues inviting in local singer songwriters from all the neighboring cities to specific regions like New York, Philly, and Atlanta to perform together under a concept called Art of Expression featuring music from Hugh from Boston, Regina Spector and Joie DBG from New York, Liz Clark from Denver, Tim Kaye from Baltimore, and many others on the circuit at that time, which was multi-media performance program that included music, art, film, and spoken word poetry with merchandise for sale so we could cross culture our arts and share fan bases. Then during the day I would volunteer with Musicians on Call in each of those cities singing in hospitals. I met a lot of great people, many of whom became lifelong friends.

Over the course of the next twenty years this would continue on and expand in over 14 countries regularly extending my music hubs internationally mainly out of France, the Netherlands, and Italy for overseas performances. And with some help from a savvy independent booking agent Inge, my international Spanish professor and then fast friend from when I had studied in Spain for college credit Birgit, and local promoters in Holland, I started supporting larger touring acts like Jon Allen, Giovanna, and landed my first opportunity supporting Luka Bloom and getting some solid radio play there. And at the same time, Italy became a second mainstay for me after meeting musician that first summer I studied abroad and staying in touch which led to returning many times and recording a vinyl record with Nicola Fantozi, touring and performing regularly there with guitarist Paulo LaGanga, making more amazing memories while performing through England, Scotland, Sweden, and Australia. With the continued help of friends and musicians in each city and country translating for me along the way, this afforded me performance platforms to share my message of resilience through music straddling international cities as well as both coasts in the US and central US namely Denver while casually meeting a birth cousin here and there, running an indie showcase in Austin for independent artists called *Spin it Indie* during SXSW all the while ultimately releasing over eight recordings all on my own. Waiting for no one to tell me I could or to help me with what I should, allowed me present moments I could never take back for a team I always wished I had but that I never did. I was used to surviving so creating a way to be was nothing new for me.

Waiting for no one to tell me I could or to help me with what I should, allowed me present moments I could never take back for a team I always wished I had but that I never did. I was used to surviving so creating a way to be was nothing new for me. Additionally, I supported myself with several jobs to acquire as many revenue streams as I could to keep myself afloat. Through licensing my music, the sales of my CDs, teaching music, English writing, and Jewish studies, excelling specifically in Jewish music education and aiding students in areas of special needs and what I would call unique learning abilities classified as special, often defined as students on "the spectrum", I learned to be an educator and a shadow for autism basically connecting all the skills I had acquired through UCLA to earn a dollar or to volunteer with any non profit that correlated with my interests including homelessness, foster care and adoption, incarceration, youth forced into prostitution, addiction, or spectrum solution solving for a difference when I wasn't on the road touring designing rehabilitation and expression programs for many along the way. A hybrid of stable home and road life was a perfect medium for my balance.

■ ■

After settling home for a while upon meeting my birth cousin Paul, I set in to assist him with his bi-monthly blood transfusions and lifestyle for a few years in order to spend as much time with him as I could simply because he too, was my family. Over time as Paul got more independent again, I started to get hungry for the road and starved for music with a purpose larger than myself and wrote a song called Listen to Your Heart coming up with an idea to partner with the non profit America's Blood Centers the independent entity version of the Red Cross, and created a tour concept called Blood Driven inspired by Paul and his situation, an irreplaceable extension of my own bloodline. The goal was to raise awareness of the value of donating blood to save a life ... well, three actually and to try and inspire people to do it.

This also would be the advancement of my fascination with documenting, as part of the tour I designed that crossed over into seven states had me visiting and performing at blood centers and blood drives while people donated blood, then visiting hospitals to perform for those receiving blood, and finally to interview and performed live for those who gave blood asking why they chose to and posting video clips of all the perspectives and what was to happen when someone donated blood and the other would received it trying to inspire all to encourage people to *"Listen to Your Heart, Donate Blood, and Save a life."*

With that, I offered a free download of the song to anyone who donated and posted about it as a creative way to generate a ripple effect and inspire others to make a difference in the world by doing the same. To my surprise it actually worked and people were getting the blood they needed and entertainment to boot. So as far as documenting and sharing went, this became my next favorite pastime to music, capturing what is in the moment for a present in the future.

When the inside doesn't match, *Underneath* the Surface.

It is also true though that despite being creative and driven in solution solving for survival, my personal life was often deeply challenged as my moods were sometimes overpowering and overwhelming for myself and others when communication breakdowns happened. Anxiety and panic would surface when I didn't even see them coming. When off stage and not singing, communicating and expressing myself would become some of the hardest struggles I faced. I did not, until later, connect these challenges to the possibility of my attachment and processing styles or perhaps lack thereof due to my early childhood development. The best I could do was work hard

on myself to manage these qualities and give my all to my relationships and friendships as I have always considered life to be a wonderful gift despite its challenges. I've often wondered if the horrors and terrors of traumas and abuse that we subsequently sense or remember are actually part from a biological biochemical makeup of sorts delivered to us through genetic DNA receptors, perhaps claiming some of them to our ancestors. Maybe Heaven is a place I'm running from. And as history has a way of simply repeating herself, perhaps it could be that awareness is keeping us awake for the healing of it all. Maybe this is why I ended up at and graduated from UCLA to begin with. Maybe this is also why I took up painting for a summer, completing over 40 paintings having never done so before. Perhaps why the search for a stable partner to create a family has been part of my life's work. Maybe it was all to complete the things my birth mother never could.   For in search of love, real true love that is, shame will never bind us.

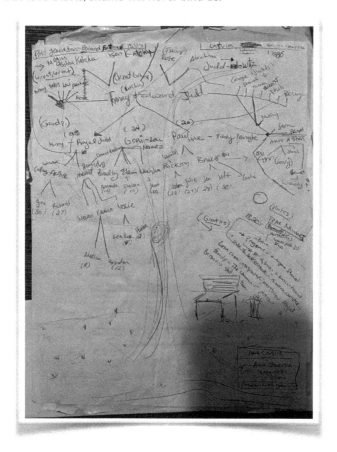

CHAPTER 6
CONCEPTION, CAMI BABY

"The sun had just set on a Friday night in early May ... after getting as high as we all could, we jumped into my brother Jimmy's dark green Pontiac and raced down ..." (excerpt by D. Logsdon)

The sun had just set on a Friday night in early May and my older brother Jimmy, Ted and Sam Nafores, and I were hanging out on Garnsey street in Santa Ana in the outdoor patio of our mother's then rented house. We had about seven or so places we lived in by that time because they were just so hard for her to keep up I guess and we would just keep getting moved. Eventually, she stayed in the Long Beach area until the end of her life with the help of her brother, my uncle, but even that place turned into a pretty full space with people coming and going around the clock, sometimes twenty or so sleeping around and about. I didn't much mind though, that's just how it was.

The air smelled of weed and hash that night as we popped whites washing them down with Budweiser beer. The older boys were talking something fierce about making music and getting some nice hot guitars of our own. After getting as high as we all could, we jumped into my brother Jimmy's dark green Pontiac and raced down to a known music shop in a neighboring town that we frequented before already knowing when they would close and what they had for us to take. Laughing and still drinking with music blasting as we sped down the road, we were ready to load up on some good music gear we had always wanted. This wasn't our first time making a small hit on a shop and it certainly wouldn't be our last, but it was my first time with my brother and his friends, and it felt a thrill to creep up to the store, blast open the windows of the shop apart with a bumper jack from the trunk, and run out with a bunch of guitars. One last slug of the bud light and out of the car we jumped managing to steal several guitars, and 3 basses, the 335 Gibson was the one I remember still to this day, before screeching away in the night.

Jimmy would later get caught due to the serial number of one of the guitars but as for me, I was scott free. As the year unfolded, my drug habits grew and so did our non violent robberies. Between hits of drugs and hits to mini marts and gas stations, we shared girl friends, pipes, and crimes the same as the fancy would dine together.

Years later, I came to discover the last place my mom ended up living in by a note on the door to her old one left by a neighbor for me to find when I got out of prison for a stint I was just done doing. See about that and all, I've been in over 14 prisons around and about California, mostly for drug charges or for not stopping my using them like the state kept trying to make me do, but man if you had to live around the people I did all the time, you'd do them too. It was just better that way and besides I wasn't much hurting anybody else, I was doing exactly what I wanted to do.

More often than not since I didn't much have the money to buy what I needed, my brother Jimmy and I would get oregano from the store, mash it down, and make fake hash from it to sell on the street for our heroine habits but even that gets you in lieu of sales of a controlled substance and you can land three years for that, even when it's fake. And we did that a lot. Overall, I've probably spent about twenty years on and off in jails and prisons until I met my daughter in 2016. And man she really did the impossible helping me get off probation, getting me gr and food stamps, a real doctor and inhalers of my own, later a mailing address and an SSI check, eventually having me stay around and about with her, and that's not even all of it. She didn't have to, but she stopped, turned around, and went back to help her biological dad.

But the two lives are totally different, hers that she shared with me and mine as it was, and when I met her I knew I'd have to choose between my life and drugs and her and her way of life because the two wouldn't ever mix. She wouldn't ever be safe. And I wouldn't say one is even better than the other really because I had my own kind of freedoms living on the street and I liked it out there.

Sometimes I even got myself caught to go to jail for a bed and the food and a place to play my guitar. And I was the only guy in mainline that was allowed to play music with all the races. Miss Bagley even put me in charge of Mr. Scully's music studio in Chino State Prison minimum yard. Most of the stuff was broken when I got there but I had gotten good with wiring and tape to get electricity from local gas stations since we didn't have much electricity around the outside area, so fixin up the prison studio and helping people record stuff was the thing to do. I loved it.

But before all that, starting as early as I can remember, I'd mostly spend my time with my older brother Jimmy hanging around with the neighborhood kids or hang around my dad's younger girlfriend Mary Lou because that's just what we did. Back in those days you gotta remember we all hung around with each other, doin the same things together, even my dad. And then sometimes he would go away for a while and it would be just me and Mary Lou. Many times when we would sit around smoking cigarettes and drinking pots of coffee between laying around with each other, she would talk about really wanting a daughter. And we all knew  my dad was done with that after already having so many kids, he even found a way to make sure he couldn't have anymore, but she always wanted to have a child.

It was around the holiday time again as December began to creep in and it was almost my 17th birthday. I had already played with Mary Lou and my brother's girlfriends before as we all shared in casual pleasures because that was the way life was back then. It was no big thing. Just weeks before Christmas, while I was still on the run from having left the Riverside Boys home a few months before without severing the time I was supposed to, my dad asked me again to stay with Mary Lou a few days while he went in for his routine quarterly check-in at Metro State Hospital for his wavering mental state. Mary Lou was used to me and always happy to see me. It seemed as though I was her favorite as she was warmest to me in our private time together. Even though she was my father's younger girlfriend and partner, Mary Lou and I had our own story of sorts, me being an excitable 16 year old looking for anything to feel good by and her being almost 15 years my senior in age but almost the same in the way we would relate to each other so we would just make out and pet for fun. The night we went all the way wasn't supposed to be by my dad's rules, but it was a secret plan between me and Mary Lou. She had wanted a baby real bad and I was happy to have a good time while possibly giving her one. I told her right away I wouldn't be there to father anyone as I was already on the run again for leaving the boys home, for safe cracking theft, for still skipping school, and for doing the drugs I wasn't supposed to do and all and it was only a matter of time when I was going to get caught to serve the time I owed. We both knew it, but it didn't stop our night.

The following morning I went off on the lookout for some whites and stole a car to get around only to get caught by the police a week later in a wild car chase that had all the cops first from Downey and then from Fullerton and then from Anaheim all in on the wild chase. It even made the news. I sped and sped in the Malibu classic I had stold and was so close to getting away. Just as I was about to exit off the 605 freeway off of the harbor offramp though, the car finally ran out of gas and spun out of control. My instincts kicked in to bend around the steering wheel in a fetal position just under the dashboard which protected me from impact from hitting the guardrail allowing me to jump out and continue running on foot. Soon I would climb over a fence and come upon a hot water shed that I thought I might be able to hide in as a get away only to have it yanked open by the Fullerton Police force with their fully loaded guns drawn at my face. The police later said they actually thought they were chasing a dangerous race car driver, not a 17 year old kid. They also told me I was pretty lucky not to get shot. That was the end of the line for me, that time running from the law, but not the end of my running from the law by any means at all as I would keep doing that for most the rest of my life until I was to one day meet my daughter again.

██

I was sentenced for two whole years in the California Youth Authority for all the crimes collected against me. By this time, my life didn't have any set plans as I was used to getting taken in. I didn't see Mary Lou again for over two years but while I was serving my time in YA, a counselor told me they were transferring me to the local Jail in LA to meet with officers there on the account of a baby being born to a Mary Lou that might be mine.

Back in those days, having sex with an underage boy was as serious a crime as it is today and since Mary Lou was already classified as a ward of the state due to still being in connection with Metro herself as well as about fifteen years in age my senior, she was looking as some serious charges for having made a baby with me, an underage boy, even though to me I was a man.

When I first met with the officer it was to be determined by a paternity test if I was the father or not but of course I already knew. At first Mary Lou had said it was my older brother Jimmy's because he was of age and they had been together in some form before anyway so it could of been true, but in the end I knew it was mine and that was that. They took me from the jail to some tall building in the Hollywood Hills looking area but I couldn't be sure, then marched me up a few flights of stairs and down a hallway to show me the baby girl. The officer let me hold her in my arms for about 2 minutes and I knew this was my daughter. What a trip so it worked. Besides, the test came back 99% positive for me anyway. After taking the baby out of my hands, she said that I wouldn't see the baby again and walked me back down the hall towards the rest of my life.

A court case ensued as to who could raise baby Cameron which was her name. Baby, baby Morantz, or Cameron as intended, though to me, she was my daughter Cameron Morantz Logsdon. But none of it mattered because no matter how many people in my family tried to get the courts to let us keep her, it wasn't long before the baby was to be taken away, and taken away eventually for good.

Now Mary Lou was classified as a ward of the state for most all of her life when I knew her, but really by this time she wasn't as much out of her mind as people thought, at least not on a regular basis, but it didn't matter anyway even though she was free from living Metro by this time because my father had been able to convinced her dad and the hospital to release her to his custody under his wing and care and that's pretty much what he did. They became partners. She supplied financial stability and he provided a sense of family though he could not give her a child for the vasectomy he had. They had something between them though and as far as I knew of her, she was my dad's younger girlfriend but someone cool from time to time to know and lay around with even later after the baby was gone. A lot of people might say she was schizophrenic and out of her mind and sure there were times where this proved to be her state, but more often she just hung about in her large flower dresses or lay around in bed, only really unstable when pushed to far to be. She loved to make a ton of coffee, smoke her Salems, and only took her prescribed meds back then. It was later when I partied around with her and my dad for years. We were all like partners really, everything was cool. In fact, I don't have a nothin negative to say about Mary Lou at all. See but it wasn't until much after she lost Cameron that she began taking the hard stuff with us. It would be five years later when she would try crack for the first time while I was in jail doing a county lid after a short stint with cocaine and from then on, she never looked back.

Anyway, when the judge asked me about the baby and how it all came to be because it was my older brother Jimmy who was in question as the potential paternal father at the time, it would of been pinned on him for the rest of his life had I not spoken out despite my age, and there was such a thing as a blood test by then to match the dna molecules and there was also my testimony. Not only that, I wanted it known that I was the father because I was proud of what I did, what I did worked, I helped Mary Lou make a baby. When asked, I told the judge it had been my idea to make sure Mary Lou wasn't gonna get in any real trouble which cost me mainline

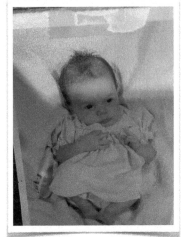

access and put me in the hole for 12 months. The hole for anyone who doesn't know is a disciplinary area of solitary confinement. That's just how it was. And it wouldn't be my last time there either, for years later I would be thrown in there again for refusing to take psychiatric drugs they were trying to make me take when all I was trying to get was the drugs I wanted to get high on and I knew those other pills weren't really meant for me. I remember also asking the judge during the case for my daughter to release baby Cameron to my mom and my grandma, even Mary Lou wrote the courts for that, which also almost worked, but in the end we all lost her anyway.

The next I heard, my mother, my grandmother, and folks on Mary Lou's side all didn't quite qualify to take the baby in so it was left undecided and she was placed in what was possibly going to be temporary foster care. By now my mother had a new set of kids Ramona and Steve by her latest boyfriend Ramon, though still married to my father for financial reasons mostly, and our fourth younger brother had recently died from an accidental self caused hanging at age 12 so the fight to keep Cameron in the family was extremely desired but a loss nonetheless. I was told that though for a while my grandmother kept tabs on where Cameron would move, showing me once a photo of her in a foster home yard on a red tricycle, she would soon after be moved several more times from foster home to foster home somewhere in the Bellflower and Downey areas not terribly far but then she was lost for a while and that put a scare on everyone especially Mary Lou's Dad Lou Lou who finally stepped in and insisted on a stable adoptive family like his far away, and so it was, Cameron was gone and I was back to living my life.

I had just been offered heroin for the first time right before getting caught stealing that car anyway, and I was ready for my new future that I was just about to fix for myself."

49

CHAPTER 7
YOU COULD OF BEEN MY FAMILY

The prison in my mind has guarded memories chaining my heart from the terrors of truths for as long as I can remember, only it's the likes of you that remind me. There are several significant men ... You may not like this chapter ...

The prison in my mind has guarded memories chaining my heart from the terrors of truths for as long as I can remember, only it's the likes of you that remind me

You may not like this chapter.

There are several significant men I can remember in my life for the many reasons why, though there were many more that mattered, let me start just before the first kiss.

I don't remember imagining to be a mother one day, though I know my birth mother had. I think for me most of my time was spent picking up the *Pieces* of what family meant.

All the Nothings

My first memories were but feelings, like bursts in the night, fear of the blackness knowing things weren't quite right. Though details escaped me for several years to come, it was still obvious - the Damage Done. What the extent I'll never be sure, but that didn't matter, the path to healing would. A uterus shifted and terrors came as they pleased, each time my curiosity led me towards intimacy. The breakdowns and shakedowns weren't anything yet, for the panic and anxiety I later met. Despite desire for love as commitments were given, most could not stay for long. For men who got close, and tried as they may, would come to know only to run. But stay as she will, hope yields to none, for all those who welcome the work to be done.

Nobody Knows
I was only two.

Heaven

Catapulted into a whole new world by age four wasn't much of an adjustment because by then I was used to moving around. Everyone was my family. Even after I got a forever home, the sentiment for me would stay true for the many people I would meet later in my life as an independent touring musician. Moving from place to place was comfortable and familiar to me. What's more was the mirror of my past in my present life as I would be on to a new host's home in the next city over just before things could crash down. Arriving at the Alpert's was like hitting a jackpot, a foster child couldn't get luckier than a room full of toys, a plate full of food, and a roof with fresh clean warm blankets to call home.

Though I had arrived with one paper bag, just a doll, a few clothes, and a pair of shoes that were too large inside, my new parents didn't let that define me. Instead they filled my new room with clothes for every season and dolls for any reason. Quickly they noticed my speech was a bit out of sorts for I couldn't recognize letters, numbers, or colors, or write and read just yet. I was almost four.

Is a place

With the assistance of tutors and persistence in school early on my parents tried to help me. Though there was major discord between my mother and me almost all the time back then. It must have been hard, what she herself dealt with growing up, but she wanted a daughter and adopted me, so here I was a picture in her life for good, for better and for worse. You bought me, there's no tag for return. School was really hard, I didn't like it so much. The numerous lunches in the library to avoid the kids throwing food at me was my only preservation. Maybe it was because they were mad at their favorite snacks being gone when I stole them, rearranging their lunches in trash cans nearby to mirror how empty their meanness made me feel. They had no idea where I had just come from. In fact, for a short while there, I actually stole quite a bit as a kid mostly from stores - cds, dresses, earrings, whenever things didn't seem quite fair, simply when I wanted something, or for the thrill of seeing if it could be done. Yet still, I fought hard to be honest and noble, and to catch up not knowing how far behind I actually was; the idiot often fighting the savant in me.

I'm running from

I never trusted many for long, women especially, disappointment always around the corner. But this was just icing of truth on the cake for my daily slice they'd dish out. Often, I could sense letdown coming as I could discern a lot of things, probably too many. Maybe it was a gift, the burden I've frequently felt perceiving things I wasn't yet told; from potential misgivings, to other people's struggles, to the negative words spoken about me by others that I could hear through the eyes of our so called mutual friends. This would happen for years and years no matter what circles I found myself in. And after a while it almost seemed easier to play right into the ideas and beliefs created about me rather than the effort it was to plow against the grain. Sometimes I'd do this simply on purpose to mirror the ridiculous once subconscious surfaced, acting out in overly direct affirmative ways to confirm what was or imagined and to help me realize that even slight bouts of disassociation for protection could never keep me locked in the prison in my mind. But eventually, I came to realize that it's impossible to conform to something you don't even see the same way.

■■

Lose Yourself Pretty Monster

I remember the first day of kindergarten like it was yesterday. My teacher was so pretty, thin long blond hair, a lengthy brown skirt with boots on, and a turquoise blouse was her work dress to teach us the wonders of the world.

The person I was fated to meet was a boy just about my height and age. We were almost the shortest kids in our class. I remember him well for his energy and charismatic born leadership style and also because the following year his sister yanked me into the girls bathroom, dressing me up as a bride for him, and pushed us to marry on the playground. The children were screaming and laughing and shocked as she and her friends dragged us closer together for our wedding commemoration. He, my only husband down an aisle as of yet, was most of all my first kiss.

Throughout the years our paths would cross, from broken bedroom window calls, to hiding him in my closet during dinner time, to sneaking out to ride bikes in the night with the neighborhood boys, to running away from my family frustrations to his house hiding out, just two kids trying to make it through the jungle of childhood in the same neighborhood, running back into one another many years later discovering we both were performing musicians. Lessons in the value of friendship, support, and longevity, a fixture for life, he would continue to always be considered extended family to me.

Everything I do, I do it for You

The exploration of boys wasn't hard for me starting with the first time I fell completely infatuated with one I met in junior high. He was the new kid and everyone liked him but for some reason he chose me first. This was new for me and I was not at all present enough to receive. He ended up doing drugs and living a whole other life completely without me. A lesson for timing with passion, we were just too young for those rolling hills.

Dark Side of The Moon, Wish You Were Here

Throughout my youth my parents sent me to sleep away summer camp both to learn more about my Jewish heritage and to have fun being a kid. They wanted to make sure I had culture under my belt and experiences to remember. It wasn't always easy, but the memories still replay in my mind extremely fondly. A lot of my identity of self was formed there. So by the time I was sixteen, I was ready to be a camp counselor and specialist, bringing with me directing and musicianship skills to share with the community there where I met my next crush. It didn't last long due to distance and childish ways but I remember him well for I gave him my youth. The hardest part was losing his best friends who had taught me to play guitar, in a terrible car crash. A lesson for inspiration, adoration, and surviving losses to come, it was he with them who opened the door to all things sonic inspiring the start of a new path in music for me.

Into the Ocean

When my first college boyfriend finally committed suicide after threatening to several times throughout my freshman year, that may of been the most overwhelming because in the end I could not stop him no matter how hard I tried. For months I had made every effort I could to console his darkened heart and tried to warn our friends to keep a look out when it became too much for only me. But no one seemed to believe my word not until the first time he tried. In the hospital, it was only me he would tell what he took, and it was only me he let feed him the charcoal that saved his life that one time. With the lessons for awareness and being present, I tried my best to be what I couldn't ultimately be for him, to hold stable ground, and one year later he would be dead by a self-inflicted gun wound.

After that compatibility for me was scarce though there were loving flares. I often wondered if love was truly really there? I was young then and decided to focus on the one love I could maintain, making music.

And that, I did.

The Nine Yards

I've always appreciated women though mostly not romantically so but if those kinds of feelings were to have surfaced it would have been this one time because of one person that comes to mind. She was funny, adventurous, warm and sincere, spontaneous and exciting. She once heard me perform live music one day at UCLA and she was so inviting. In just a few days I would be traveling West up the coast for my first time on tour, with two songwriters I had invited with me (I wasn't a very attentive driver back then) and could use all the help to maneuver. She came to my house, jumped in my car at the last minute and came with us even though we had just met. What I came to discover was I could not be her lover, I wasn't even quite sure completely why yet. During that trip we watched a film that began to reopen my mind, dark memories and blurry thoughts I couldn't make out for some time. And any attempt at tender touch would trigger in me cloudy visions to much, terrors inside with a chain that would bind me, and in the end she was better my friend so that nothing more would remind me of what the cause of that was.

Here Comes The Flood

I've come to conclude that you can love many people throughout your life, sometimes at the same time even, for all the different reasons *Underneath the Sun* and for every other way they may make you feel about yourself and even for the ways they didn't make you feel at all.

I don't recall myself to ever really be disloyal, on the contrary rather, smothering for love with an air of demand for the reciprocation of it. But it was all in good heart and the best I could do as a survivalist knowing nothing but perseverance. I will admit, however, that my tolerance for tumultuous waned to none as the years kept on in webs of co-dependence and convoluted connections that began to ail me until I stopped seeing spiders. Only I didn't even know really what that even was, for confrontation and overly directness became a protected cloak that began to fail me.

Sing Me Home, There Must Be Some Kind of Way Outta Here

Then one day just out of college I met the one who left an impression that still lingers from time to time like the melody of a song. Loud music blasted from the apartment complex I lived in at the time and all of Westwood could hear him play I was sure. My first instinct was to shut it down and low and behold his front door was unlocked. So naturally I let myself inside. Lost in a whirl blaring Jimi Hendrix guitar solos as he was one of his favorites, this guy was a really good musician. From then for a time we were inseparable. As moments passed us by together, it was he who taught me most about guitar and playing it, moreover about connection to love, but soon the terrors regularly would begin to surface and everything quickly began to unravel apart. We split for good in different towns, but the music would often rewind us. As the years would pass, I didn't want to let avoidant attachment keep the best of him. What I remember most about him though, beyond the independent touring up the West Coast I would bring him along for or the terrible tricks played on me by him that I tolerated, wasn't even the late nights where I would sleep as he would rise to record songs in the middle of the quiet nights, *Day for You*, nor was it the arguing and odd jealousy I wasn't mature enough to foster kindly for him. No, what I remember most was his efforts to see me and accept me as I was when he could. In the irony of his attempt once to rearrange my bathroom items trying to help me hang a butterfly art piece one afternoon and me screaming but I have an order to things, to where they belong...... both of us looking back at the bathroom in disarray to anyone else's mind, me then seeing the look on his face as he glanced back at me sheepishly, and how the both of us just broke down into inconsolable laughter. Because in irony, he saw the real me and let it be so, and I appreciated him deeply for this. He even told me years later that it would be a shame if I wasn't to become a mother, that he knew I would be a good one.

Those words never left my heart. I don't like to fight, I don't need to be right, but I needed to be heard and understood, *Help Me Out.* Yet there was such a dichotomy there for he had also felt disconnected with the Jewish heritage in me and ultimately ran from it all. How was I to understand this or why and it hurt so much to feel rejected and denied because of whatever "it" was. Years later, his apology confirmed for me where my once budding love of loyalty had been hurt so deeply and somehow I was still coined as a 5150 for my pushy initiative and aggressive ways, but I knew in my mind to take it in stride, and not let that perspective cloud or define me. At the same time for me, there was something deeply comforting in a hug with him that always reminded me I would be alright. I was so excited to reach back out and share years later when I discovered the other half of me was actually English too, and maybe not so different after all. With the lessons of healing and growth, safety and space, lessons to give and lessons to take, though *Those Times Are Gone*, what I saw and loved most in him was a man able to look deep inside himself, grow, and evolve, and make a mistake. Persist.

It wasn't meant to last despite our harmonies, as the harmonious dynamic of mature man and woman lacked just enough for it to become a pastime instead, a once was 'we' withered away despite how safe he could make me feel. Those long ago memories live now, and While You Wait, just like yesterday, in the melodies and rhymes are echoes of old songs, and from time to time I'll still play them when the stereo is on.

Like melodies that refuse to fade, heard faintly in the shadows between the light, I only screamed louder for consistency, communication, and kindness even with the worst of me just to be understood, but I would just find myself caught Below Sea. But when a gift is in the giving, you might be surprised what you get back.

In Your Eyes, Breaking Down

The hardest was the man who seemed to have seen me as someone to keep, as he chased me to change me, the story far from neat. There was no Release Me, we had chemistry. When we first met, he, nine years older, I 23, but he was married with two young children and struggling so. We met at a music venue we were both playing music in and I heard in his playing the kind of passion, dynamic, and sensitivity that I imagined his person exactly the same. I instantly wanted to make music together. It was a tumultuous Hurricane with the most alluring eye of the storm, and before one year up, it seemed we couldn't be separated from one other, meant to be one, but not meant to be. *Ain't that a Shame.* I was told it was over, I waited a year to move forward, but I had no idea the complications he would face there, unraveling more of my dark deepest fears. He separated from his wife on and off for many long years to come and she took his children away from him across the world, forever wounding him alone. Cadillac, Negroni, Kettle, and wine, always pressed reset to make everything fine. The word would go dark sometimes for days, I couldn't see, or breathe, or find my own way. The electricity drew me and drowned me in what others coined lust. But for me, I was just elated at the sensation of feeling fully freed by approach, I no longer engulfed in ocean of touch trauma waves of distraction, but I would always starve for more and a different set of tides began to trickle in. I would never formally meet his growing children, kept separate, I was. And all too often it was too much to keep going to bat for me, for the road to hell was paved on good intentions apparently. By now I just wanted to Fade Away. Demanding what I thought was true love, anxiety and panic surfaced and simply took over. All I had wanted was to be a family, and to share in the milestones that came with it all. *Body and Soul.* But it was never meant to come to be. And in fact, many of those years are blank and forgotten as the panic attacks became my main mode of being and got the best of me for quite some while. What do you do when someone you deeply love disregards you and doesn't inform you in a language you understand over half the time because they aren't present somehow or able to do so? Was I the catalyst, the cause, the crutch? Probably all, but for nine long years the trauma for everyone was too much, though I really tried at love. I know he did too, he did a lot for me. Most peculiar was when I came to learn the name he shared with my birth grandfather like the man my birth mother came to love and wished for a family as well. Neither she nor I would end up with a family of our own by almost the same age, another coincidence? Probably not. But the lessons from this were eternally long, faith, loyalty, and word of mouth can be interpreted wrong.

All it Takes, **Waiting for the Sun**

The break up for almost three years, add that to the nine, was the break up that wrecked me and was my lowest time. But from there I was helped and built right back up with the support of a new courageous man who tried to instigate my growing up. He did his best in trying to heal my deepest wounds. Day and night for almost two years he kept at me, showing me burgers and beer, days in adventure, life beyond tears. But like oil and water and because I was far from ready to receive him, I soon was to discover what panic and anxiety truly was and why they haunted me so as our dynamic began to trigger and unravel the deepest darkest memories forgotten in my mind.

Being locked outside of his place to avoid my compulsions to see if he was really still there during the many silent shut-outs to Pavlov my brain triggered a fear of being left so deeply, even I was surprised. I began to remember now in pictorial form all that had been forgotten. The foster home door steps I was placed outside of alone when I was sick at age two, half focusing on a red tricycle to stop myself from being ill was one that came to mind. That wasn't the only memory that began to surface either. But who could blame him, it was I that would show up unannounced uncontrollably and inconsolably to check if he was still there. The anxiety became panic, the panic became attacks, and I started to become afraid that I might never come back. The only thing left to do was leave.

Needless to say that relationship didn't work out either but the lessons to Face the Beast and One of These Days fully transition completely granted me my relationship to myself and the deepest part of healing began.

Even When It Rains

Then here was the best friend always there through the strife, taking me in, sharing with me, silently listening and adding to my life. Adventures, and meals, New York an extension of self, the lessons of humility and patience in the art on the shelf.

Until Then

As anyone else may experience, attachment can be strong so I returned back to the man I once thought was the one. I really just wanted to be family. But when the hustle and bustle stops you really get a chance to take a look at how much you actually love your life, what really fits, and what doesn't. It didn't work out but if it hadn't been for meeting him, I might never have found my birth father.

Simple Mood

Welcome, you have now arrived at the most profound lessons in transformative love. If only you could follow me Where Lovers Go. *Take it All*, what you will, and kindly leave the rest.

POSTSCRIPT HOMELESS, THE WAR; ADDICTION ONE CRISIS

Currently, LA's annual homeless count, released Friday, shows that 66,433 people now live on the streets, in shelters and in vehicles within the county...

Homeless the war. Currently, LA's annual homeless count, released Friday, shows that 66,433 people now live on the streets, in shelters and in vehicles within the county. That's up 12.7% from 2019. Within LA city limits, the number of people experiencing homelessness is 41,290, a 14.2% increase over last year.

Most people see homelessness as a personal tragedy affecting those who cannot afford the cost of renting or owning a home. But why, in the early 1980s, did so many Americans find themselves homeless? Why did the accumulation of personal tragedies reach epidemic proportions at the same time across the nation?

The answer to these questions is rooted in both large-scale economic and political forces, as well as increasing personal vulnerability. Four interrelated dynamics were at play: declining personal incomes, loss of affordable housing, deep cuts in welfare programs, and a growing number of people facing personal problems that left them at high risk of homelessness

Leaders first considered the scope of the problem in the 1980s, when L.A.'s homeless population began to swell — particularly around downtown. Despite some temporary measures, the city struggled to address what it acknowledged was a major problem.

In 1982 the homeless moved under the freeways coining themselves as "the Troll Family, part of the growing tribe of homeless men and women who dwell in the concrete caves formed by the thousand or so bridges over the freeways of Los Angeles. Others started to camp out in the shrubbery along the freeway landscape.

In December 1984, advocates for the homeless opened a temporary shelter downtown at 1st and Spring streets, in the shadow of Los Angeles City Hall.

Nicknamed "Tent City, " it looks like a battlefield hospital.

In the spring of 1985, a homeless encampment known as Justiceville sprang up in a children's playground at 6th Street and Gladys Avenue — a ragtag compilation of plywood, cardboard, tattered blankets, old tires, discarded drapes and about 60 homeless people.

Ted Hayes, who organized the place and gave it its name, said the makeshift dwellings in downtown Los Angeles allow homeless people to take care of themselves, and he has challenged government officials to work with him to come up with a better plan.

As the homeless situation got more dire, the city took some dramatic action. By 1987 As police continued to force people off skid row's streets and sidewalks, officials signed an emergency agreement for a temporary "urban campground" for 600 transients on 12 acres of vacant land near the Los Angeles River.

In 1991, a change in the population started to grow and the city began to divide the homeless into thirds.

— "Have-Nots" are the upper third — without jobs, without homes, but without other problems. They can be helped quickly.

— "Cannots" are disabled by drugs, alcohol or mental illness. They can respond to treatment and may benefit from help.

— "Will Nots" are the bottom third, the sidewalk campers who will not work, the derelicts and deranged who will not seek shelter. They, say some, cannot be helped Just this year 2020 L.A.'s Homeless Population Grew 13 Percent Since Last Year's Count and now it's everywhere from the city to the valley and everywhere in between.

Addiction, One Crisis

Sociologists, educators, economists and psychologists know that yesterday's homeless were down-and-outs, beggars and vagrants, lazy bums and the romantic hobos. The vast majority were white, elderly, ill-educated, alcoholic males.

Today's homeless are a full slice of society and include college graduates, single-parent families with children, Vietnam veterans, professionals, businessmen, former politicians, ex-crack cocaine addicts and teenage runaways.

Hope of the Valley

With the push from the mayor and an extreme for change, "we needed to come up with new strategies, structure, and funding. Obtaining partnership and funding changed the landscape of what we were trying to do in improving the city's homeless situation dramatically. Van Nuys has always been the epicenter of homelessness in the San Fernando Valley and we wanted to create a one stop shop where anybody in need can come and get a full array of services whether it's a hot meal, a shower, clean clothes, case management, mental health services, veteran services, so instead of someone going to a shelter then being sent out to somewhere else, we would provide a space where it's all centered in one area. In providing a place to avoid patient dumping where hospitals would simply dump their homeless patients back on the street, we devised a series of platforms for all types of transitional situations in need." Ken Craft, Founder CEO Founded in 2009, Hope of the Valley Rescue Mission began as a small ministry run out of San Pablo Lutheran Church in Sun Valley where volunteers cooked and served hot meals to homeless men, women and children.

(Pic: with Laurie Craft as guests and volunteering at their annual Thanksgiving Bash the first year we found HOV in 2016)

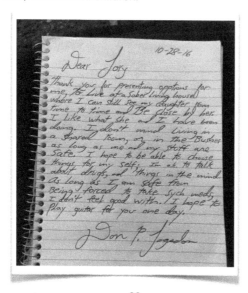

(Pics: 2016 dropping by birth father off for an hour at the HOV Van Nuys Help Center to explore it while I ran errands when we first discovered the grounds by chance in an AA book. He got a shower, a hot meal, an AA meeting, and to play chess with some locals.)

After several years and hard work by 2010 Moved to a 26,000 sf facility in Sun Valley and began providing showers, life-skills classes and case management.

Each year after that things progressed quite rapidly, opening John E White House recovery for men, Genesis House a 30 bed facility for the homeless, opened our first enterprise thrift store in Granada Hills, then opened The bridge a transitional facility for men in Canoga Park.

And by 2014-2015 we had taken over operation of the Los Angeles Homeless Services Authority's Cold Weather Shelters in Pacoima and Sylmar with a total of 290 beds, Opened our second social enterprise Thrift Store in Santa Clarita, and Relocated our homeless services to Van Nuys, expanded services and named the program the HELP Center.

And our growth didn't stop there.

In 2019 we converted the BRIDGE program to a 38-bed shelter for youth ages 18-24 in Burbank called The Landing, opened Shepherd's House, a 48-bed crisis housing program in the West San Fernando Valley for homeless families with children, opened 2 50-Bed Cold Weather Shelters in Antelope Valley, opened a 48-bed crisis housing facility for homeless moms and kids called Casa de Vida located in the West Valley, opened a Safe Parking shelter in Palmdale for 30 cars, Launched a weekly Motel Meal Program to address hunger issues of the more than 400 homeless families living in motels in the Valley.

(Pics: 2016 - my birth father Don trying out a temporary transitional sober living home endorsed by Laurie Craft of Hope of the Valley just before I came to realize in order for a full transformation to work for him, it would be best done directly with me - all or nothing.

By 2020 we opened an 85-bed NoHo Bridge Housing residential facility in North Hollywood called Tiny Homes, opened the NoHo Navigation Center in North Hollywood where clients can take showers, store belongings and access case managers and housing navigation, opened the 100-bed Van Nuys Bridge Housing residential facility in Van Nuys, and opened a Work Ready/Day Labor.

Spread out over 12 facilities: We now have 170 Family and Youth Beds, 138 Emergency Beds, 185 Interim Housing Beds, 13 Recovery Beds and 30 Safe Parking spots. Our mission is to prevent, reduce and eliminate poverty, hunger and homelessness. We do this by offering immediate assistance and long-term solutions. We are a faith-based independent nonprofit organization that does not discriminate based on gender, age, ethnicity, sexual orientation, religious affiliation or lack thereof. Our services are grounded in a deep respect for the dignity inherent in each human being.

(Pic: Three years later with Laurie Craft of HOV after a lunch time concert at the Center)

(Pic: Three years later with HOV founder and CEO Ken Craft after performing and spending the day at Hope of the Valley Van Nuys Help Center during their annual Thanksgiving Bash)

Our vision

is that no one goes without...

Hope– A message of love, support and freedom for a better tomorrow.

Hot Meals– Food distribution to the hungry.

Housing– Emergency/transitional shelter to the situational and chronically homeless–

Health Services– Resources for basic human needs.

Healing – Proven programs that lead to wholeness and self-sufficiency.

At Hope of the Valley we believe that everybody and everything deserves a second chance and choose to focus on the spiritual, emotional, physical, relational, occupational and financial needs of our clients.

Be with the change, Be part of the solution with Hope of The Valley.

Some Resources:

Recycled Resources for the Homeless

Hollywood Food Coalition

Multi Purpose Center (LB)

Downtown Women's Center

LA Works

References:

Hope of the Valley: History

LA Times Article: Homeless Retrospective

KCET Article: The Rise of Homelessness in the 1980s

LA Curbed Article: Homeless Population, Los Angeles

(Pic: A. Spending time getting help with resources and collecting information at The Multi Service Center in LB where ultimately a fews later they helped us obtain SSI for my birth father. B. A few years later meeting one of the board members, David Dubinsky, of the Hollywood Food Coalition at their Christmas Meal Offering for anyone in need leading to shadowing Don with volunteering and performing together at their space. C/D. Performing and Speaking at for Recycled Resources and Hope of The Valley with my birth father Don)

PART TWO
PROLOGUE - "PAWNS DON'T GO BACKWARDS"

"I'm just trying to blue print my beliefs so people don't misunderstand me so much" .
D. Logsdon

"We are a reflection of how we are educated"

"I'm just trying to blueprint my beliefs so people don't misunderstand me so much"

"Relationships won't get off the ground if it's only one way. people try to steer it in only one direction they want it to go instead of see both sides.

You have to sit down and talk about it and look at both sides rather than one person take over. you would have to map out your entire dreams and wants and desires not wants and all that and the two of you would have to sit down and map out what you both want let you see it and talk about all that."

"I find them physiatrists to be just as crazy as the mental patients themselves"

"Homeless is supposed to mean that a person can take care of themselves on the outside of this world"

"You done did what you can't undo"

"Pawns don't go backward"

~ Don Patrick Logsdon

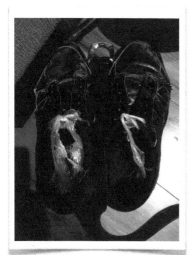

CHAPTER 1
BELT OF TOOLS (FOR THE HOUSE OF SANE)

By now I'd been through so much... this new chapter would eventually turn into the most amazing moments of my life. This was when I learned for the first time, that my birth father ...

By now I'd been through so much therapy and to about every which kind there was out there, so it seemed, that I could almost claim the hours spent for my own possible mental health professional career if I had wanted one. That is, if that could have even been done. I'd be the first to tell you that I've tried every mental health term on. Did I border the line? Certainly adhd, Could it be spectrum? Aspergers subtlety? Perhaps just anxiety? I didn't have answers but I related to each of the distinctions every time I would have a great falling out. There started to be quite a cabinet of files. Turns out a definition didn't matter much, for it's all in the awareness, curbing, and management of the behavior that is

you, and that's a commitment for a lifetime. I'd finally reached a comfort level with having faced and accepted so much from all the lifelines connected to me that seemed to inform me. At least I had gained a plethora of life skills, knowledge, and tools though, time well spent, time not wasted, and I was ready to change my life.

After having imagined myself as every race, every ethnicity, and every mental health frame relating to my dispositions to discover where I may of come from, I grew tiresome of focusing anymore on my adopted self and began to look outward instead. And low and behold, being defined in a box does not always serve us. Nonetheless, in order to reach understanding and connection, the inner discovery towards self aided me well and helped me to develop my tool belt for life that held knowledge and experience to use when I fell. This could be used for any situation that may come up for me and I would later begin to show others when to pull each tool out to get through anything. This tool belt was best used for what I would define as the Mental Wellness Spectrum, and the reward of response when each tool was used inspired more ideas of creative solution solving approaches to manage and work alongside it. Wherever one may fall in the spectrum on any given day, could in fact use a process of preferred approach with creativity leading the way.

As it turned out, these concepts I'd mind map on my walls during the middle of the night were about to become part of my life's work.

First I digress.

In 2011, a friend of mine from Mexico got arrested while in a domestic fight here in the US and sadly he was convicted of more than one felony due to being here without papers. To support him through the loss of his freedom and soon the larger loss of ever obtaining status in this country, I took it upon myself to visit the Los Angeles DA to try and help his case with a lesser sentence. Eventually, when that proved not to be enough for the crime of staying here illegally, I sent him books and letters and visited him in prison for a year before he was deported back to his country. His situation inspired me to write a transitional assimilation program using tools from my belt woven with the fine arts for the men's correctional facility in downtown LA, and to my surprise the Los Angeles police department accepted my outline, walked me through the jail to see all that was there, and to show me where the program would be implemented when someone could volunteer to provide it.

Though I had already spent a lot of time in downtown LA volunteering, performing, and devising programs of progression on life skills and social integration for the Downtown Women's Center for the homeless, already familiar with the area, this was my first birds eye view inside the California Prison and Jail facilities, which unbeknownst to me would be one of the few insightful life experiences that ultimately prepared me for soon meeting my birth father.

The second collection of insights would be discovered from a personal bad choice I had made, a mistake in which panic had again taken over and ended up leading my way.

In 2012, while at a hotel bar on what I thought was a meeting for music, after several drinks - more than my body could handle, it started to seem that things were beginning to take a dark and suggestive turn. As a red flag went up despite how drunk I was, I ran from wherever that night might of taken me, yelled for the valet and demanded my keys jumped into my car and fled from the scene.

Driving wasted is a terrible thing and it's lucky I didn't hurt anybody. And when I saw the red and blue lights flashing behind me as the black and white pulled me over, it was in that moment when everything clicked slow motion into place, it was as if almost extremely familiar and something I'd already faced.

For some reason, I just knew deep inside this was supposed to be happening and soon enough I would find a whole new path in life was about to unfold for me. I wasn't an addict or even a user interested in drugs, I wasn't an alcoholic or much of a drinker but sometimes my frontal lobe seemed like it was. Yet, the most profound of lessons come when we least expect them.

That summer was really insightful and taught me a lot. I learned to identify feelings and to accept the things I cannot change. I came to discover where all the AA meetings were in the city and how to manage panic with what I now call protective brain pause. I learned of the laws and more on the court system too, so when I would finally find my birth father homeless, using, and running from the law, all these life experiences I had in my tool belt guided me what to do.

Add to that summer my private time spent working with unique learners as a tutor on the side, often with students with learning challenges or on the spectrum of autism. Inspired by this I spent lots of pastime studying the brain and personal responses to creative solution solving suggestions I would provide. In fact of my tutor students in particular had responded quite well to an idea I tried. He struggled too much with anxiety when required to write long papers on a computer being that he couldn't see the pages that he wasn't working on and his brain would get jumbled and freeze. So I came up with an idea I called the Rainbow Box Theory to help him see. The idea was to take the number of shoe boxes that matched the number of paragraphs and lay them out all across the floor, having him color code each part of the paper infrastructure so he could write some more; topic sentences - red, transitions - orange, important phrases - highlighted yellow, paraphrasing - green, quotes - blue, explanations - purple etc. He was then directed to drop his ideas into each box whenever they were to come to his mind, actively placing the different written sections into the boxes where they belongs avoiding brain stops. He was finally able to write out of order creating works of rainbow in each one later pasted together from pieces.

To my amazement personalized solution solving suggestions per each unique situation worked towards positive results.

Paralleling my both my creative and professional lives, this process to success also became the inspiration for the title of my first music album Pieces which sonically engulfed the process of arriving at self by collecting and putting together the many pieces of our lives.

Now, with all of these creative approaches stacked in my belt of tools, looking back, perhaps I was subconsciously preparing myself for if I was to finally find my birth father. For somewhere high on a shelf in my closet for all those years sat a file of me with court documents I had been holding onto since after my mother's death. Inside was a list of information and stories that I hadn't fully processed yet.

And printed in there was his name.

By now in my life my relationship and dreams were becoming a sinking ship and I starved deeply for something so much more and began to crave for it. Could it be that the missing pieces of me would lead me to finally being able to cultivate a family of my own one day?

It was the fall of 2015 when I was handed a new packet of me filled with addresses,

numbers, and a few notes in it with more history. A private police investigator in the family of my soon to be once had been partner had taken the time to help me. Through my birth father's social security number there had been an address attached to where a mail trail had been, which was about to give me a start in reconnaissance leading me to go *undercover in the field* to find out more about him. The PI was nice enough to track all this down for me from the other side of the country with simply a name. I was amazed.

For a few months, I secretly roamed the area taking notes of observation at first, for I was not going to just enter a situation unprepared - especially one where everyone warned me to avoid in order to protect me. I researched the crimes, the arrests, the drug lines, I researched the gangs, the streets, and the ways of the world there. I took notes of the exit routes closest to the metro and planned a plausible way in. By this time my relationship had finally failed for certain and it was time for me to focus on creating something steady. I was now free, curious, and open....... finally I was ready.

Without a preconceived notion or plan at all, except finally able to present for each minute that was about to unfold right before my eyes, this new chapter would eventually turn into the most amazing moments of my life.

This was when I learned for the first time, that my birth father Don was actually still alive.

CHAPTER 2
MEETING MY BIRTH FATHER

... pointed to a sleeping man on the ground, his belongings scattered about; a partially broken tent over his head and he said, "Here you go: this is Don, your biological father."

A Few Months Prior

It was early evening on a Thursday in November, the later that year in 2015, when I called a phone number listed in the packet the PI had given me just a few months before and heard the voice of my paternal biological grandmother for the very first time before. Though I didn't reveal who I was, I finally was able to ask the question I had been wondering for so long: "Is my biological father still alive?"

With her answer being yes, a breath escaped my lips and all I could do next was hang up the phone. She would pass away several months later just before I was ready to call again so I never met her. But that was all the push I needed, time of essence now, to go to find my birth father.

By this time in my life, I had just returned back to Los Angeles from a six month stint working on music splitting my time living in Nashville and New York City, making a live record with mixing engineer Rob Matson and Guthrie Trapp on guitar then driving back and forth between cities to meet with Steve Greenberg of S-Curve Records in NY about eventually licensing it after planning to have it mastered back on the West Coast by my favorite mastering engineer Eric Boulanger. But as soon as my songwriting mentor AJ Masters passed away from cancer alone the exact night I had decided to leave his home early for my routine drive to New York after having been staying and writing with him, I decided to move back to LA, at least for a while. And when my third attempt at another chance in love once back in LA started again to fail, it seemed time for me to focus on something different - maybe learn more about myself and where I came from to figure out where my life should head next.

On a whim, prior to getting the news that my birth grandmother had passed I drove by the several of the addresses listed in the PI's research that documented where people in my birth family had once resided to mind-map the path of my paternal bloodline past.

I also discovered in the notation that my birth mother had once lived in a few of the dwellings too, even passed away near one, and through deductive assessing between the court documents I had and the packet from the PI, I came to realize that I had even been conceived in one of them listed there as well.

The final address on the list correlating to social security numbers documented the most recent place of my living paternal relatives whereabouts. I still was very

hesitant to open a door to a part of my story that so many people were urging me to keep locked, the first time I drove past without stopping.

Over the next few months, I occasionally wondered how the people in that dwelling were doing, and moreover, who in fact they really were. One morning, I felt a deep nagging inside of me: the thought "you must call that number" would not leave my mind. For a few hours, I called and called but to no avail; no one answered. Being that I'd always been a very intuitive person, something about her not picking up felt wrong to me. I searched through the legal documents I had obtained from the PI to find another phone number and I called it.

The person who answered told me that my biological grandmother – who I had spoken to just months before - had died, but that my biological father Don, Uncle Jimmy, and a half aunt, nephew, and half uncle were still alive. I was told that they were all to be avoided, labeled as unwell outsiders still embroiled in legal issues involving crime and drugs.

That phone call could easily have been an indication to walk away from all of this, but instead it motivated me more. The very next day I got on the Metro with nothing but a house key and id, dressed in a plain shirt, with a sweater for warmth, and my bell bottom jeans; I got off the Metro at the exit that would take me to where some of them lived.

■■

My Uncle Jimmy

I walked up to the house and there was a man outside cleaning. From a distance, I couldn't quite see his face. Could this be Don? Or maybe it was my Uncle Jimmy? I thought to myself, Is he dangerous? I decided that criminals can't be imminently dangerous and threatening if they are in the middle of cleaning stuff up, so I approached. He glanced my way briefly then returned to his cleaning up.

I asked softly, "*Are you Don?*"

"No; what do you want?"

"So would that make you ... Jimmy?" I knew from the court papers he must be one or the other. This made him stop in his tracks. He looked up at me but he hadn't figured out who I was yet.

I realized that I was about to enter into all of my biological family's lives without any indication yet if I'd be granted their permission. So I asked, "*How would Don feel if he were to meet a family member of his?*"

Jimmy replied, "*What do you mean? What kind of family member? We know everybody in our family...*" His voice trailed off and he squinted his eyes so he could look at me a bit closer.

Before he could say anything more, I said, "Well ...yes, but do you think that Don would be okay with... I mean how would he feel about.. you know, I just mean... would he be ok with the idea of meeting his biological daughter?"

Jimmy didn't miss a beat. He said to me, "Wow - you're Mary Lou's kid! Come in, come in!"

And I did come in: deep in this dark dwelling was a small space for the living just beyond the dead. Hidden in the darkest of darkness of this hallway were 24 sets of cat eyes, stacks of music everywhere, and music posters and drapery along the wall. The drapery and a collection of crates separated the hallway into two makeshift bedroom areas. And that was just once side of the space.

As I waited for Don to arrive, I listened to Jimmy's stories for hours, quickly discovering his musical talents and that he – like me - was left-handed. I learned that my biological father was also an excellent musician. Living as a musician, I had always suspected that my talents were in some part a biological inheritance: now I realized that they most definitely were.

Jimmy told me some stories about his and Don's childhood, constantly assessing my intellect, awareness, and assessing my understanding. I later discovered he had intentionally left out certain harsher details of my biological father's past that he wasn't sure I was ready for. I found his concern and care for me particularly touching. But during this first visit, Don never showed up.

Breathe, Dust to Dust

I returned to visit with Uncle Jimmy a second time, sharing with him selected pieces of myself but never revealing my legal name. I offered him some more information about what I knew about my biological family to encourage him to open up to see if his stories matched what I had read the legal documents I had seen. They did. This established our first line of trust. Hours upon hours I spent there with him sifting through photos and letters while he blasted heavy metal songs for me to hear, and a deep bond began to form between us. In one letter written by Don from jail to Jimmy that my birth uncle showed me had me in tears for when I read through the lines with the misspellings of words, I could sense that my birth father was actually a kind intelligent human being. I also learned that my birth father was very much a free spirit; in love with the freedom of the outdoors; such a deep contrast to much of the rest of his life, as he was most often locked up incarcerated for petty and grand theft, as well as numerous drug-related crimes. For Don, living in the bushes between casinos or under freeway underpasses meant that he could double his welfare money and take his drugs in privacy. He later told me that he equated this freedom with the most incredible peace of mind he had ever known. Yet, as much as I enjoyed this time with Jimmy, I had come to find Don, and still he was nowhere to be found.

On my third visit, early morning July 26, 2016, Uncle Jimmy had new information for me. "Don is in the back. He is passed out sleeping, but soon you will meet your biological father."

I couldn't believe it. I was nervous and excited. I was ready.

Meeting My Birth Father Don

My biological uncle, Jimmy, led me to an outdoor dog run on the side of his house. Jimmy pointed to a sleeping man on the ground; his belongings scattered about; a partially broken tent over his head. Jimmy said, "*Here you go: this is Don, your biological father*" and he walked away. I sat myself down on a crate and I looked into the eyes of this man who was starting to wake up, - my biological father. Trash spewed all over the place, a broken tent showered over him like a creative umbrella, but charmed I so was as he rifled through piles for his glasses in order to see who I was.

The first words out of his mouth to me were: "*God Damn you're beautiful!*"

Don: "*The night before, I was living across the street from a casino and getting high in the bushes. I went back to Jimmy's house where I get my mail and occasionally sleep, and I passed out. When I woke up and opened my eyes, I was looking straight at my daughter.*"

All my life I had so many names, yet in this moment, I had to figure how this man might relate best to me. I had been named Jennifer ever since my first foster home when I was an infant but I didn't much care for that name. And for my whole life after that, I had been Jenni or Jen, Cindy and CJ, Tasmanian Texter, Menorah Jones the Jewish version, or poofnic the poof. But when Mary Lou, my birth mother died, I discovered that she had wanted to name me Cameron, and I wanted to honor that too. I had always felt that there was something a bit different about my past and my journey; as if my past ties had hoped my future would become more than they could provide me with. Now sitting with my biological father for the first time in my life, I realized that there had been a moment 30-some odd years ago, when I had been placed into the arms of a 16 year old ward of the state – my biological father - as Cameron, and that would be how he knew me. That moment must have seemed to be forever ago for him, and maybe for me too. That moment was what I had been chasing to understand my entire life. I decided before revealing my legal named self and all that was attached, to call myself *'Cami'* a nickname for short, not too different from Jenni, to offer him a familiar name to see what he might recognize in order to connect together - before sharing much more about me.

"Hello, I'm Cami, your biological daughter." I said, but I didn't have to say a word more, because the moment our eyes locked, we both simply just knew.

Don: *"I was a seemingly irreversible drug addict. I used heroin, cocaine, crack cocaine, methamphetamine, crystal meth, and pills of the worst kind you can get your hands on: Oxycodone, Demerol and a lot of others. As a retired grand theft criminal-turned-petty criminal, the only crimes I would commit at that time would be things like stealing from a shopping mall or a grocery store, like a couple of jars of coffee,* food products, flashlights and batteries; odds and ends that I needed because I didn't have the money to pay for them. I needed to stop but it was either do without those things or steal, and my choice was to go about getting them the illegal way. In addition to that, I was on the run from my probation officer because I couldn't pee clean and stay sober, so I was in hiding and always on watch to see if any authorities were anywhere around and about looking for me. All of that changed when I met my daughter. Looking at her for the first time was like looking at about 78% of heaven. It was like an electrical charge; very much like a bolt of lightning of unbelievable and unexplainable happiness. That's what it was like."

From that meeting on, I considered my time with Don timeless. We had no formal boundaries to speak of, only insightful parameters I slowly laid out as we got to know each other. There is was no schedule or plan. Time simply slipped by us as we relished in each present moment we had with each other. I began through observation and conversation to learn the details of his current life: he was running from the law and was very close to facing the possibility of being put behind bars again and what I didn't yet realize quite possibly for the rest of his life. If prison did not take him first, there was a very real possibility that his addiction to hard street drugs and narcotics would. This did not overshadow the possibility that I recognized in Don which

was the understanding of a type of love he did not yet know could exist between two people, but a love I wanted to give and decided to offer.

Don: *"I thought that she was going to say, "Hello. Maybe we could take a walk to somewhere and get some coffee and donuts" or somethin. I figured that she would be checking out what kind of a person I am and that she would come to the conclusion that I'm not really worth too much of hanging around for very long. I really had nothing to offer. And then I figured she'd simply say, "Well, maybe in a couple days I'll come by and see you," and then she would just get in her car or however she came and leave and not return for weeks, possibly months, or ever again at all. That maybe I'd see her once in a great while after for only a few minutes. If that would've happened I would've thought that sounded normal. But instead, what in fact happened is that with each passing day she returned for another visit. We started to care about each other and like each other which actually happened right from the very beginning - within the very first minute of our introduction really. That first day turned into hours and as the hours turned into days and one day after another was going by, we started opening up to one another. Cami would sometimes even find me late in the night and bring books in a funny little blue backpack for us to read. She had these interesting games we would also play so that we could get to know each other. We started talking about things that we like and things that we don't like. And then we started to feel more and more close it seemed.*

I never had this type of experience before, except maybe with Heroin...."

CHAPTER 3
SUPPORTING MY HABIT

"If anyone were to read my Olson files and learnt about all the things I done in my life, they'd think to themselves no wonder this guy sticks to himself, who in their right mind would wanna hang around with him...." (Excerpt by D Logsdon)

The World, A Prison Out There

"If anyone were to read my Olson files and learnt about all the things I done in my life, they'd think to themselves no wonder this guy sticks to himself, who in their right mind would wanna hang around with him. And for anyone who doesn't know that is, Olson files are a secret stack of files in a government database related to each individual person who has ever done time in the penitentiary system named after the court case that established the right of people to view their non-confidential prison records. (That last part my daughter looked up [Prison Law Hand Book]. We weren't much

informed on a lot of stuff about our rights back in those days). I learnt a lot while I was in the prison system, over and about in and out of 14 California prisons and jails to be exact over a time period of 25 years. This would start when I was in booked in the juvenile system, continue through to California Youth Authority Correctional Facility, graduating to Jails and finally to prisons where often you would be moved about mid sentence depending on what you did and how much room there was for you. The first prison I went to was after I was booked on a felony for sales of narcotics in the form of the drug hashish. They start you for two months in reception. I was in Chino on the East Yard, booked on the 13th floor in dorm 9 on bunk 43, and then I was moved to CRC, the mainline prison for my first time. I was 26 years old.

How come I was never a person who never had a job in the outside world? Never in my life did I do that before, had a regular job, wake up in the morning and go to work 9-5. There simply was no way to carry on with all four things; a drug habit, gambling and selling whatever I could, and buying dates to be tied to a full on job. I couldn't stand the thought of it - it didn't make no sense to me, I'd rather go throw myself in jail first before living in the prison of that life.

Habits

When I was twelve I used to sniff gasoline for a high but after a while it was making me feel out of control and not myself getting me lost walking around the city and unable to control my body similar to psychiatric medications so eventually I looked for another better high and quit doing that. It's really important here to understand that I quit because I wanted to quit, not because someone tried to help me quit or because they told me or forced me to stop. An addict will change drugs from one drug to another or find another thing to do when and because they want to. If they are ever in a position where they are forced to stop because they absolutely have to, there's a good certain chance that at some point later they will start up again. The only way an addict who is truly an addict for whatever the reason in their brain will only stop is if they actually want to. See if a person is a drug addict they are one because of one of three reasons. One is someone introduced drugs to them sometime in their life and after they took it they actually

liked it and so from then on they go carrying on with getting high because they enjoy it. Reason number two would be if someone got spiked, slipped a drug they didn't know much about by someone one to physically and chemically addict the person first which leads them to needing more without them even realizing it, like a doctor or a pusher who is willing to risk the felony, to create the habit. The third one is if you are outright born that way where the need to get high is already part of your brain and you brought that need into the world with you. Also there are two types of addicts, one who likes being one and one who doesn't but they cannot quit because they are physically hooked. Now the second type would be a good recipient for a halfway house, recovery home, or even jail as a means to get loose from using and then AA programs would apply to staying off. But if you have a person that likes getting high and doesn't mind having a drug habit, then such a person would not benefit from AA because they aren't interested in the first place. You can't force help on someone that don't want to be helped. Now the thing is even when or if an addict stops one thing - the drug or a particular one, they will go and find something else to fill that empty physical or emotional feeling. It could be anything, even caring for a non addict, and then they would stop using to have the relationship since they can't have both. But if there is nothing else in the world to substitute it, the habit will always come first

Heroin

I was 16 was the first time that I used heroin. It happened one day in Fullerton when I went to go buy a dime bag of weed and the connection needed the $10 I had so he could score a $25 balloon of heroin with it. Once I realized that, I told him, "well I'll tell you what, I'll give you the $10 to go with your $15 you got to go get the bag of heroin, but instead of giving me the dime of weed I wanted a third of the bag instead" because I was looking for every drug I could get. I already

had done just about all the other kind of drugs you could think of, uppers, downers, alcohol, marijuana, lsd, speed, and there were only two drugs left I had not gotten a hold of yet, were heroin and cocaine. Of these two drugs, heroin would come first.

Somehow my friend Kent agreed to give me part of the balloon and cooked it all up with a needle and spoon then he produced two hypodermic syringes. He filled one of them up to about 50 units and the other to about 25 units showing me he had the correct splits for us. To this I agreed to continue the deal so I offered my right arm, tied a bandana around it, and Kent plunged the needle in my vein and injected the drug into my arm and it was an extremely incredible high. So much so that I would continue using $10 shots every other day for the next two months, that grew into a habit that would sometimes cost up to $150 a day for a thirty year period of time.

In early May a few years later, I got out of YA and realized right away that I was gonna need money for my drug habit and the girls I was running around with at the time and this money was gonna have to come from somewhere, where it came from was gambling casinos. It just so happened Commerce, Bell, and Cudahy were just finished building one down the street called the California Bell Club, and later they opened the Commerce Club, the Bicycle Club, and the Normandy Club. Everybody in my family knew how to gamble in every game you could think of, so I picked up on it and right away learned how to win. My main games were poker high ball, poker lowball, craps, black jack, and roulette. My routine would be to make hashish out sage and sell it for cash then head to the connection to buy heroin and later also cocaine, saving a small amount, about a quarter or so, for gambling at the casino. With my wins I said for females and food while living out of the Miller Hotel. On the streets the girls were doing their thing, and I was doing mine, so eventually we worked together in order to protect each other's business. My hustle was selling hashish, their hustle was selling sex. So what we did was we went out together at the same time so that we could put our money together that we made and buy harder drugs and split the costs of the weekly motel. I wasn't the type of person that would carry on a love affair due to knowing I was going to go to jail. I didn't want to have a problem of them waiting for me on the outside world so I would tell the girls "when I get busted you are free to go your own way and find someone else" because it was too much of a heart ache and too much of a problem to carry on with a relationship with me being in jail and her being on the streets.

Inmate D17670

Throughout my twenties inside of every twelve months an honest precision of two thirds of my time, which is about eight months, was served in LA county jail; Biscailuz Center and Wayside Honor Rancho spent behind bars that didn't yet involve a state prison. Pretty soon I would start seeing the same people I did time in Juvenile Hall with. After the first time I was booked into State Prison, D17670, it would go from that point on for seven to eight years on and off for windows of time as short as two weeks and as long as sixteen months-2-3 on drugs cases alone. In between these stints, I started to get released under orders to report to the probation officer located in Huntington Park, about a three mile bus ride from my motel, for anti-narcotic drug testing weekly and was directed to get a job. Due to being in the criminal system I was limited to certain types of jobs in assigned places though, farmed back into Los Padrinos Juvenile Hall to work there as a cook until found out that I myself had once been a convict in there so they had to transfer me out because you can't mix and mingle with the people you did time with inside there. The same thing happened to me those three months later when I was then assigned to Metropolitan State Hospital in the laundromat because I had also already spent lots of time there with my dad and Marylou when they lived there. I had the same problem and ended up losing both of those jobs. See, people in prison and mental hospitals are not allowed to have contact with anyone working there from the outside world either because then you would know the people. I just kept losing jobs and it was too much to make every meeting with probation all the time, and besides anyway, I had my drug habit to take care of. And for that reason I made drugs and hashish and sold the stuff to finance my gambling and drug habit.

My Home Outside

By the end of my twenties living in homeless hideouts where I built my own dugouts near freeway off ramps or hidden around railroad tracks closest to casinos was the most ideal place to live because it costed less money than paying motel bills plus I couldn't tell the probation officers where I lived because they were always looking for me to arrest me. I had access to an address connected to my mom every time she would move, which was a lot because she didn't have that reliable of an income and would get evicted a lot, but I liked it actually better in my homeless hideouts outdoors. My Uncle Don would throw in the first and last month's rent for each place leading up to one called the King Aquia Apartments in Santa Ana after she had already lived in three other places in that city after have left Bell Gardens having moved from six different houses before that.. This would only be in a five year period, while my dad and Mary Lou would live at The Apprentice Hotel on 7th street and San Julian in downtown LA. From there she would continue this pattern living in Fullerton, Anaheim, and back to Bell Gardens within the next five or so years. Eventually my uncle would buy a small pad in Long Beach for my mom to stop. All the moves but most of that place got sectioned off, filled with stuff to the ceilings, local transient people and the gangs that needed a place too.

The Advancement of Charges

In 1990, I got discharged from prison and went home to Bell Gardens and found a note the door sayin my mom didn't live here anymore and her forward address was located somewhere in Long Beach on Ximeno Street but there was on house street address written so I walked around the neighborhood and ran into my middle brother Michael fixing his moped in the driveway. My older brother Jimmy had a similar history as I in the systems and and wouldn't get out himself to join us until three weeks later.

For most all of life, I was hanging around and partying with my older brother Jimmy. It was the best relationship relationship anyone could ever hope to have because he was my partner in most everything we did. We got high together, we made out with the same girls together, hung around with the same gang member together, we were bandmates together, and committed petty theft crimes like stealing pop bottles, then bicycles, then tools, clothing, shoes, then pickpocketing together. We even had nicknames for one another. His name was Wizard and mine was Star Leader for the band we had made together. I also called myself Manhattan Don when I got out the last time I was in because New York was where I wanted to head and a guy on the yard said I looked like a Manhattan Don, and I likded, cuz that place was always a dream of mine. By this time Jimmy had about six months left of time to serve but the same day of his release we met up, scored a balloon of heroin and got high together. This would go on and get more involved for many more years but so would the crimes as well. We even stoled a car together once and went all the way to Las Vegas to gamble. We made out with about $7800 and even saved a pregnant cat before we were to get caught and flown back to LA to be booked on charges for absconding, possession of heroin, sales, and smuggling.

One night in October around 1991, while we were carrying on with our lives as drug addicts, Jimmy, with one of his prostitute girl friends who had been recently stiffed on a date, went down the street to talk to the guy who refused to pay. Jimmy and the girl rushed back to get me to go with them to try to help get her money with the idea to rob the guy also which we actually went back with intention to do, but we never had the chance because after knocking on the door that was already slightly open while walking in, he produced a pistol and shot Jimmy. The bullet went in Jimmy's abdomen out his back and right into my ass. We ran back out into the street where a buddy of ours gave us a ride to the hospital. When we got released from the hospital from the gunshot wounds, we went back to his apartment with our prescriptions in handwritten from the doctor at the hospital for our gunshot wounds that he caused to get him to pay for the narcotics. The landlady answered the door saying he wasn't there and offered us $4 so we took it and we left. But tis would lead to our arrest of which the charges would now be suspicion of robbery and assault with a deadly weapon based on her version of the story and since we couldn't afford a lawyer we got a public defender and lost our case, getting six years for a bunch of crimes we didn't actually even do in the penitentiary.

But I just kept thinkin of all the stuff that I did do to chalk this one off.

Playing Guitar and Recording In Prison

While I was set up in prison, and this time for the long haul, the regular odd jobs I was assigned to in the kitchen as an OD cook for the cops, wouldn't be allowed this time. The

warden here told a bunch of us that in order to get any kind of job in this particular prison that we would have to go to school, and they cut off all of our long hair which really a messed up trip because it was the first time in my life to have short hair and mine never grew back. So now I had no choice but to do everything they said, for the prisons had changed a whole lot. I was forced to go to school, and even though I couldn't spell or write too good, I ended up getting my GED while I was in there. Also the drug trade in prison was all dried up and monitored now so I was stuck with whatever I could get in trade. Meanwhile, while on the Solano minimum yard, I saw some band equipment in the dormitory band room and told the guys that were playing their instruments that I knew how to play too because I didn't have any other job I could get. It turned out, I knew how to play better than they thought and I was granted a pass to play blues, rock and roll, oldies, and salsa jazz with all the different bands put together by the different races, the only man on the yard allowed to do this. We would play huge concerts for the convicts, often me, setting up stages and wiring the equipment. Miss B, the lead sergeant of Entertainment on the yard, ended up giving me my own jail cell, my own amplifier, my own guitar, access to the recording studio called Skully's recording studio, and all of that went on for 19 months. The deal was to make a cassette tape for her which I did. Later, when I would repeatedly get busted again for others under the influence of drugs cases while running from probation, she would let me back in to continue making the music I made. Sometimes, I would even get busted on purpose for a bed, some food, and to play music there.

The King's Rook

Back in the year of 2010, every convict had to go through a psychiatric session for two weeks and the only way out was to prove to the counselor that you were not crazy. See, at that time one quarter of the population of the California Prisons equaling 33 prisons, were mental patients that were not supposed to be in there but they were there because the mental hospitals had been closed down due to overpopulation. Well you can not put mental patients and down syndrome on the mainline with everybody else because the mainline convicts will start a riot. So what the authorities did in order to get rid of these mental patients is they locked up everyone in prison for two weeks and prove you weren't crazy yourself. So what I did was brought my chess set, a deck of cards, a pair of dice, and a drawing of a roulette wheel, and played the games in front of the counselor of which I won in all the games and said "Can any stupid person who is either crazy or down syndrome do what you just watched me do?" He realized I wasn't crazy or down syndrome so he let me go. This hadn't been the first time chess had saved my life.

Checks the Balance

Many years later, on a Wednesday in the afternoon while I was out on parole for possession of narcotics because I got caught high again, I went back to one of my hideouts in the alley near my mom. A guy hanging around came up to me there and asked me if I was Manhattan Don claiming he knew me from around. I thought he had been a guy I had gotten high with so I let him sit down. He said hey man, "I've gotta problem here, I got a check with no Id with no way to cash this thing, can you help me?" So I said, "As a matter of fact I can, I have an Id."But you gotta know I never had a bank account to my name in my life and never actually before set foot inside one. Then he said, "Here go cash this for me, and I'll give you half the money" so that's exactly what I did believing it was a real check. If I had known it was a bunk check I never would of gone inside. But when I walked in the bank to try and cash it for him the cops pulled up and took me in. Later, my mom told me that after I took the hit for that, he went back to my area with a pick up truck and a couple of guys and took everything he could get while I got booked into prison for another three years.

When the judge saw me for this he took a look at the write up and told me to my face that he knew that I didn't commit this crime, he had booked that guy in for setting other people up before and recognized him. I didn't even know how to commit that kind of crime or that I was breakin the law. While I was sitting in the bullpen looking at 14 years waitin for the judge to decide, when he realized I didn't even do it, instead cuz he had to give me somethin, he gave me my shorter sentence.

The law thinks that if you are a criminal you will commit any crime, but they are wrong about that, even criminals have a line that they won't cross, crimes they won't commit. Half the time people plead guilty to all the charges against them because the public already believes you did it and they realize they are gonna be found guilty anyway. You might as well have as much fun as you can until they come and get you; there is actually nothing you can do to keep yourself out unless you're lucky. The one thing that kept me sane while I was in prison serving all that time was realizing that I wasn't the only person in there for nothin. Doesn't matter if you did it or not if they wanna lock you up they are gonna do it. There's a lot of screwballs out there and we gotta share this world with them. If drugs had been legal, I would never of been a criminal in the first place.

Crack Revolution Sustained

In 1994 strikes were to come into existence and it would be drawn to my attention that I was on strike two, three strikes and you are in for life. Gangs moved heavily into our area and had already began taking over the garage of the house my mom lived in, now in Long Beach, cooking up crack and other drugs while running a prostitution racket for money. Now, back in the late 80's crack became just another drug on our list. My teeth started to get loose and all messed up so I pulled them out one by one by myself, the prison doctors finished the job, and got me some dentures but they were too big so I ended up throwing them out. And by 1995 we all would be doing crack now and often we joined up with Mary Lou who was still around, as she was already into it for ten long years herself, already having been introduced to it back then by different gang. But one early morning in April, that year after everyone, all night, had been doing their thing, she took a walk outside in between hits, and her heart would suddenly give out and she would die. This scared me so bad and it was a really terrible experience that I left that area for a long while. My life after that mostly consisted of gambling and shooting up while living in the bushes away from the gangs and the police. Though I would infrequently return for my mail and to say hello to the remaining family that lived there, nothing really ever went back to being the same. My drug habit and problems with the gang members there only grew deeper each time I returned.

Until the day I went back to see my remaining living brother Jimmy to say hello and for some money when he told me the news"

He said, *"How ya doin Manhattan Don? Your daughter came round here looking for you."*

CHAPTER 4
I'LL BE YOUR HEROIN(E)

Since I came to arrive at this stage in life with a special skill set to handle Don's challenges it seemed the perfect time to put those past experiences and tools to the test. But I was never out to save anybody....

Belt and Cloak

Since I came to arrive at this stage in life with a special skill set as Don's challenges unfolded one by one, to see what new options we could create for all he was facing, it seemed the perfect time to put those past experiences and tools to the test. But I was never out to save anybody. We for some reason we're lucky when more often others aren't so lucky, because for some sometimes addiction is just bigger than any one person. It

just turned out that the timing was right and the connection between my birth father and I was mutually positive and symbiotic support for the both of us.

From having spent so much time in my past having volunteered extensively with those experiencing or choosing homelessness already spending months roaming the streets with the homeless women of the Downtown Women's Center with the field trips I took them on to inspire them, as well as having had written that rehabilitation program for the men's correctional jail - among the many other things that shaped my youth, unbeknownst to me at the time these experiences would ultimately prepare me with ideas and outings with Don. It occurred to me now that perhaps for all of those years, I had been unconsciously searching in the shadows of every homeless person's eyes to get close to something my biological parents had experienced. And that all of the things that I had done up until this moment in time really did seem to equip and arm me with the awareness to be open to creative approaches as this relationship unfolded. It would be deeply exciting to see Don's continued positive responses to all of the creative solution solving suggestions I devised for him to try as he began to experience so many new things with me. This, coupled with a desire to truly learn who this human being was, spurred me on.

In order to visit Don regularly in Long Beach daily from my then downtown LA residence, I had been taking the new LA metro for precautions, dressing extremely plain and bringing very little on me; some water, some cash, an id, some house keys, and that was about it. And to carry the few necessities I had since I didn't want to bring a purse or anything of value on my person, I decided to use a small backpack I had found in a thrift shop specifically designed to hold needles and meds for those struggling with epilepsy that had visible badges on it noting to the public what it was for, which I found extremely interesting. Upon research online, I made the choice to buy and wear it on me each time I went into 'the field' where Don was, which really was a dangerous area, almost as a  protective cloak because I discovered while reading that many of them also knew based on their own criminal experience how extremely serious of a crime holding more than one felony with a very long sentence attached if they hurt an epileptic like that. So to bring it along seemed like a worthy idea to me. And my whole time out there on the streets with Don while I wore it, no one hardly bothered me. I'd like to think my protective cloak pack had something to do with that.

Notation, the Medley of Our Adventure

As I started to spent more time with my birth father, I began to observe him and keep a journal writing down the activities Don and keep a journal writing down the activities Don and I did as well as keeping track of his drug use, highs and lows, to better equip myself daily of his habits, with who he was, and who he might want to be. I also asked him his thoughts about the things we did in order to keep a sort of log of his progress and perspective. I'm not really sure why, while in the moment, I decided to do these things as none of it had been preliminarily thought out, but our time together was going so well as it was intriguing, and he seemed very interested as well. It wouldn't take long for me to also realize the depths of Don's situation and I wanted to keep him safe and more time to know him. He was attentive as a sponge is to water for all the new things we explored and each activity seemed to provide positive outcomes with him, so I kept the adventures going. I would show up at different times of day to observe and try to evaluate his lifestyle, track his drug use, noting the interval between using, and how his personality and mood shifted based on his use. I also made note of what things felt like home to him and what things felt like freedom for him.

But a rival drug gang who began to notice my visits wasn't too keen on my presence believing me to be either a high end prostitute or worse yet an undercover narc so they had their eyes closely on me.

Now, as creative and thrilling of a time we were having, we were outdoors with the homeless and gangs so trouble was expected to possibly unfold agt any time so I was as prepared as I could be in any given moment, just in case. There were a few discerning times when danger lurked closer than either Don or I had liked but that just brought us closer, motivating Don to consider changing his life so we could be safer together.

One late night while Don and I were hanging out sharing stories with one another, a gang member from that other gang popped his head over the alleyway pointing a brightly lit flashlight into our eyes. We both knew he was armed and was trying to see what we were up to to check up on us. It seemed he was looking for something, if not trouble, and the best we could do was stay calm. Eventually, Don bought some drugs off him to get him gone, something he often would do I observed.

Another time when we were driving to get some coffee and a snack on a night after I finally started bringing a car down with me, a police helicopter flew overhead shining lights from the sky to find someone or something they were looking for. Don got so spooked he jumped out of my car and dropped everything he had out of his hands scattering all in the street and into the dark he ran. They weren't looking for him that time, but it was at that point that I realized how serious of a predicament Don was actually in. When things calmed down I grabbed all his things and brought them back to him in the shadows of the alley. We were somewhat partners now, and he needed his things. I asked him if there was possibly a safer way for us to continue hanging out for him to come up with some ideas. The one in particular to turn himself in started brewing.

Inject in the Pivot

There was also time when he snuck away to the nearby garage for a few to buy a hit of real crystal meth to settle his fix and to make sure the gang members in the nearby garage by the alley attached to the dwelling kept their cool. As he slinked away into the night saying he'd be right back, I snuck right behind him out of the alley and followed him to observe so I could keep informed of all sides to the reality. He bought a dime bag of meth and proceeded to hide preparing to head back to the area for his syringe. I snuck back to my seat on the ground pretending to wait for him. Now, I had never seen drugs like this up close let alone anyone take them or do them myself, but I didn't want him to hide or pretend to be who he wasn't and what's more is I wanted to note for myself the details of his daily plan; when he would take drugs, what he would take, when he could come down, how much that he needed, and how often so I knew who he really was. I wanted to know him just exactly as he was while introducing and sharing things with him so that he would be comfortable to have as much out in the open as possible. By this time in Don's life luckily for me, he had already stopped doing heroin for a few years because of the expense, which would have changed the outcome of our story dramatically if that was the drug he was going to try to kick, but he was still choosing, and he was still using, and he was still an addict.

He came back to the spot where I was sitting, very distracted, seemingly ready to head somewhere for a bit (I assumed to shoot up), and while it may seem absolutely counter initiative, I stopped him and said *"You wanna shoot up? That's what you do right? Well, go ahead, don't mind me, do what you want, do what you need to do"* and just kept sitting there. He just stared at me for a long hard second, shrugged and said ok, then proceeded to wrap his arm with a band and get under way with his needle. I had also sensed for a while the place was probably tapped by the police who had been staking out the area for a hit on the big dealer, so in some ways I felt watched and protected and safe enough to decide to go with my own instinct even if it seemed crazy and was actually illegal. And if it wasn't, well then I must have had an energy bigger than all of us on my side. I sat there as he proceeded to shoot up but it was extremely anti-climactic for him and after that he never shot up a lid in front of me again. In fact, he told me a bit later that he had he disliked so much how it felt to have me there with him to watch, someone he was starting to deeply cared about valuing my experience and safety, that it became a turning point for him as to why and how he decided to stop using heavy narcotics and street drugs, and stop for good.

Don: *"I knew pretty early on this girl my daughter was society's child, and didn't do anything bad, no drugs at all. And in order for anything to work between us the drugs would have to go, both together wouldn't work. Neither would running from the law. What she didn't regard was she was hanging around with a felon who was wanted and as long as I kept this life up, she would never be safe."*

■■

Creative Station

The minutes together that we shared in that alley those first three weeks began to turn into hours, which then turned into days. In between walks, donuts, and deep conversations, we would sit and read children's books together so I could note his reading, processing abilities and of his desire to learn.

Then one day after he proudly showed me his electrician knowledge and electronic skills, wiring up batteries together to better light the area and fusing together a speaker system to listen to some songs he liked while enjoying some terrible instant coffee together, an idea came to mind. I decided after having logged Don's drug habits for several days if there was another yet similar option of something to get high and excited about that he could bond over. The closest thing I could relate to with Don was my intense love for coffee, espresso, and caffeine. So I bought a travel wagon on wheels, visit a Home Depot store, grabbed a car battery, a portable stove burner, and all my coffee and espresso paraphernalia, selecting beans from each known drug country separating and labeling each including sugar and creamer packaging each on in ziplock baggies and brought this portable caffeine station right to his space in that alley. My portable battery operated craft coffee cart on wheels was ready for my new connective experiment. I rolled into the alley with all this in tow and waited for Don's high to come down to its farthest low as I had documented it, and proceeded to set up this creative station for exploration of highly caffeinated coffee all powered by the car battery for him right away. It was so awesome, that even the local gang members stopped by to drink some and thank me as they began approving my visits which continued on for quite a while.

My biological past began to intertwine and embed itself with the present moments Don and I were sharing as he would share stories of his life with me. Connections, similarities and an unbelievable sense of fulfillment ran through both of us, an alluring electrical current bonding us in our time together. My instinct was to let every moment we shared unfold naturally led by the impulse of whatever made sense, but more than often I felt a deeper energy guiding me. It was profound. I was also surprised at Don's openness and willingness to spend time with me so quickly. Not once did he take any money from me or ask anything of me. On the contrary, he was extraordinarily giving, open and excited to do whatever it was that was presented to him.

Don: *"I quickly realized that by just sitting back and letting her do what she wants to do, I'm winning and she's winning and that all makes sense. Here was this person doing things and getting involved in my life, and this was bringing me a type of happiness that I've never felt before. And then I felt an attachment to this person. I really started to get attached to this person. This person indeed was my daughter."*

■■

Final Turning Point

One night in between visits about two weeks in while I was back at home for a few days, the longest I was away, I started to get this real nagging feeling inside of me to go and visit Don right away. The feeling came on so heavy and strong that the time it usually would take me on the metro seemed too long. For the first time I jumped in a car and got there as fast as I could as late as it was, and kind of by fate for when arrived he was actively overdosing from being sold a bad batch of crystal meth. I gave him my jacket and gave him my socks and asked him if he wanted me to take him to the hospital. After he threw up all over the ground and helped him to relax so he could come down, he chose to rest outside there in the alley.

When he woke up then next day I had returned to help him clean up the area and walked him to a nearby laundromat and to my surprise he didn't actually know how to use it. After we washed his bedding and some of his things we still needed to clean what he was wearing so I asked him if he wanted to walk down to the beach since there were no showers and he mostly used buckets or toilet bowls, using the ocean seemed a lot more comfortable. So he followed me. When we arrived at the beach, we entered the water together with our clothes on; this was one of the most profound rebirthing experiences we both may ever have had. And in fact, I think this was the final turning point for him when he finally decided to change his life.

Don: *"On the night when I almost overdosed for the eightieth time in my life, nothing new for me, my daughter just happened to show up. Kind of a good thing because I had just been sold some bunk dope and she kind of saved my life. Instead of leaving me there like I thought anyone would do, she actually stayed and helped me. When she came back the next day she came back and took me to the laundromat and had me wash my clothes there for the first time then dragging me into the ocean with her and a bar of soap to clean myself off which was kind of a rebirth in a way, I started to think this girl was something super different than others and I started to not to want to let her go. No one else had ever done such nice things for me. Not anywhere like her anyway."*

Family Fun Field Trips Begin

After that close call even though the local gang started to fizzle away and seemingly get busy with other things, I decided to mix our routine up a bit and started to take him outside of Long Beach on what I would call *'family fun field trips'* where it seemed safer and was new presenting opportunities to see him outside of his element in the event that transition away from street life would one day be an interest of his. We did many fun things during the first weeks I spent with him and I began to stay with Don for longer and longer periods of time.

We started to explore areas of downtown LA and he showed me all the spots he would chose to set up his world to live alone outside but to him they were his homes, hidden away from everyone under freeway on ramps usually placed near the commerce casino to double his change to get drugs and food for the night. He also directed me through all the neighborhoods where he grew up and told me stories about my birth mother and his past, telling me pretty much anything that would come up. We also began taking day trips to the downtown public library and

even went to a museum. We ate BBQ, with him insisting he pay for his own meal and saw a live music show. We even spent a day riding the metro to explore the Los Angeles area in general where I showed him a recovery facility that I knew of which also happened to have a recording studio on its premises. Then he told me that he had been to so many in his life sharing the stories of oppression and sadness he had experienced there, which instigated why he would run. Taking more notes and processing all I let each day naturally unfold as I began to see a larger picture from his perspective on what may or may not work if he wanted to transition towards something different. The truth was he had been exposed to and experienced so little in the realm of opportunity and creative support that a change in

outcome would never come to transpire for it would never be able to sustain. When back in Long Beach, we started to seek out more peaceful places outside of his normal routines, found a neat craft coffee shop called *Lord Windsor Coffee* to do craft coffee tasters as the barista was real nice to us, and shared a we love for the English theme, and day or night we also went to the beach a lot, that was our favorite place.

Don: *"She came over every day and started taking me to the library, and out to lunch and dinner - places I've never been before. She also brought this coffee thing on wheels and showed me different types of coffee beans making coffee for us then later took me to a really nice expensive coffee shop and introduced*

95

me to a type of coffee I've never drank before in my life. And then there was the day when she pulled us into a senior living home that had a black big piano in the window. She sat me down and began to play for me and the seniors in the hall and I nearly cried. I couldn't believe how incredibly good she was at playing and singing these songs she said she wrote. I had no idea she was that damn good, It was really something. Not but a week later and my favorite moment together was when Cami brought me to LA and allowed me to play guitar with her at a music show she had. For the first time I saw all her original cds and the music name she was known under. She was opening her life and her world and her music to me and it was something really incredible. To play music with my very own daughter was like finally having the band I wanted to have; and like having the family I always wanted."

By participating in Don's life night after night and day after day, I also came to fully learn of the serious dangers that followed him living on the streets and being surrounded by drugs, gangs, and crime. Though I knew this is how he was used to living and that he has survived just fine on his own all this time, I began to value his safety and life and inside me grew an instinctual desire to spread a protective energy field around him.

The Depth of a Man

Also in these first few weeks, I got to witness a man of his depth and intellect discover for the first time the high you get from espresso and watch him enjoy the new things I'd introduce him to with more joy than I had ever seen. The contrast between his willingness to spend time with me in order to get to know me was in stark contrast to his drug and crime life. The chasm seemed so vast, and it didn't take me very long to see that his spirit had never been exposed to so many of the things that I was fortunate enough to experience when I was adopted that now I was starting to feel committed to sharing with him. I also came to discover quite quickly that on the contrary to what others saw, Don was actually generous and kind. A highly intelligent thinker, with a remarkable capacity to retain information and collect information in order to apply it in such a way, I believed he could eventually be inspired with talents and guidance to play a part in how I often tried to live my life as well, with a value called tikkun olam - which is helping make the world a better place with talents and life experience. The more time we spent together, the clearer it became that there was a specific reason why I wanted to know the depth of this man: there was a heart of a spirit in him that no one had ever come to know and I was somehow granted the privilege to see this about him and it was truly amazing the first times I did. I came to know it as fact and it didn't take long for me to realize how much love I had for this man. I knew him even though he didn't raise me. He was a part of me and I was a piece of him. He was my biological father, the person who gave me life. Why shouldn't I help him with his?

It also seemed that Don enjoyed being seen as a kind of father figure when I shared personal things, such as my desire to start a family myself. He wasn't the 'father that I never had' because my adoptive father Bill played the role of father perfectly well. Rather, as I took an interest in guiding Don, he took an interest in guiding me too. And this symbiotic bond would eventually unfold into the most profound journey together both of our lives had yet to experience. I learned more and more about who he was before we had met and of his bravery and survival skills that inspired me so – as he let that other man of himself slowly go and embrace who he was open to becoming - it was remarkable.

Ironically, but not so unusual, seeing this new man emerge began to mirror to me all the kinds of qualities I would want to see in the type of man whom I would want to fall in love with and maybe even marry one day. He seemed to help me get closer to what compatibilities I should be keeping an eye out for.

Morningside

Don: *"I kept thinking that after a short while of her being with me after we met - like maybe a few days at the most – that she would get tired of walking around with me and being around me and that she would start thinking to herself, "Well, he's a nice guy and all that, but I gotta go. I can't be just running around with someone like this." But in actuality, the exact opposite thing began to happen. She began showing me all sorts of new things and an unconditional love instead; I didn't even really know what it was. This is what won my attention. I have never had unconditional love before in my life ever and I truly started to love her."*

CHAPTER 5
JOURNEY OF TOGETHERNESS

In those early first few weeks of our reunion there were so many adventures that unfolded each day as the hours together increased, but there was one in particular that seemed a pivotal turning point that led us to a new step forward....

Trial Transitions

In those early first few weeks of our reunion there were so many adventures that unfolded each day as the hours increased, but there was one in particular that seemed a pivotal turning point that led Don towards a new step forward. One day, week two or so into our reunion, I decided to blindfold my birth father, (point being so he wouldn't know where I lived or how to come and go), to see how he would do inside a warm home with clean sheets, and a shower, and a hot meal

too. This was his first time ever in a fresh clean healthy space, with everything in order, nothing out of place. I washed his clothes as he showered and gave him fresh pjs, shaved his face and trimmed his toes, and invited him to stay. I gave him the bed, made sure he felt safe, tucked him in real neat, and observed his humble gracious heart as he quietly fell to sleep. The morning after I set up the kitchen with food and tools for him, showed him how to make french coffee and he showed me how he would make breakfast. It was really amazing to see how this man would act and feel inside a home with me. But the activities themselves though new and special to Don wasn't actually what got him truly thinking about new ways to live.

Extraordinary Measures for an Extraordinary Man

It was the decision to blindfold Don that would be one of the most significant ones I would make for the next two and a half years of our journey to come. It was so different from any common way of thinking and doing, for some reason Don really appreciated the idea and the way my mind worked, perhaps a mirror of himself, a daughter he created. It was kind of like the childhood trust game, as I built routines and parameters for us as Don would let me lead and guide him into the different places I lived at the time, all based on trust. It later would become clear to me that one of the reasons our dynamic was working was because I was not only starting to act as his advocate in the processes of obtaining the things he needed for more stability in his life towards self reliance, but I also became his social skills 'shadow', a term used in the spectrum world, providing social and emotional skill set direction and guidance for all the new situations Don began to find himself in, a role I learned and developed during the years prior to Don when I spent time working as a tutor and a special needs social skills shadow for the autistic students I helped and it was Don that would actually let me. It wasn't so much that I felt Don needed experience exactly, but I felt that if I offered him guidance with introductions to what he had never experienced or had before, and if we did this together, perhaps his perspectives and interests would broaden. As the days would pass into years, this is exactly what did happen. In a way we were parenting and healing one another for all the days we had missed with one another.

Don and his Intelligence

Don is extraordinarily smart in his creative survival solutions and by no means incapable, but his approaches would often vastly contrast what society may recognize as appropriate and successful and I wanted to protect and redirect him with that.

In fact, in the early days, sometimes Don would revert to youthful behaviors as a way of relating with me, speaking in a soft childish tone or extremely loud to be heard but instinctively I saw these behaviors as as positive social inexperience protection self preservation and because he was used to being misunderstood and disregarded rather than something qualifiable for a mental diagnosis. And although over the course of his life he had been assessed with having many different possible clinical issues throughout the course of his life, as I observed Don more exposing him to new things under the veil with consistency and kindness, I began to believe he operated in the ways that he did more due to a combination of what he had and had not been exposed to throughout his life as well as the drug use and treatment inside the institutionalized environments he was placed in, less than solely due to a chemical wiring and I wanted to reach him by trying something different. The ultimate purpose of blindfolding idea was to avoid him seeing the routes to where I lived when I as I would take out of his natural environment and assimilate him using mine to always keep my life slightly separate, safe and intact just in case anything changed.I didn't tell my family, my friends, or the relationship what I had been doing either, and this wasn't to keep them in the dark, rather it was a way to protect them from their worries or preconceived notions they knew based on education, and because I wanted for the first time to be able to follow my instincts, trust my own judgement, and experience my journey in my own way. I knew from education that addicts often would return to their old lifestyles and to their drugs of choice, and even steal from you wreaking havoc in your life, so I also didn't have a set of expectations or any ideas of grandeur when inviting Don into my life. I still wouldn't advise anyone to get involved with a situation like ours without field experience and external support as our dynamic was extremely unique and special to us. Don would remain registered homeless despite the fact that I continued to shadow his life indoors and outside feet from where I would reside daily throughout the rest of our relationship together simply to always leave the door open if he ever wanted to return back to his old way of life on the streets but he never did.

Our First Music Gig Together

Don: *"After spending so much time with Cami, I started to think what life might be life if we continued this way. She was listening to me share so much about myself, I realized I hardly knew much detail about her but little by little I was part of her life. She was smart like that. Then the most amazing thing happened. walked together around Long Beach like we usually did and she decided to pull me into that home for seniors that had a nice big black piano in it. All of a sudden, she began singing and playing the piano for everyone and this was the most incredible thing I ever heard. For the first time I realized she was not only a musician like me but an extraordinary one."*

Then she invited me to perform guitar with her at her next show up in Hollywood. I couldn't believe it. This was so stunning to me that my daughter was this good, a professional musician, something I had always wanted to be. It was also a thrill when we drove up to this place called Genghis Cohen where she was to perform to a packed house. First we checked the sound of the guitars together and then she sat me in the audience for the first few songs before she called me up to share our story and have me play my guitar.

I sat there and listened and couldn't help my tears, she was really really good and so were her songs. If my dad and middle brother were still around, they would of been proud. After that night my mind was irreversibly made up that from then on I would change anything about myself I could to carry on this relationship with this young woman who was actually my very own daughter. When I was watching her play and sing on the piano that afternoon I thought I was watching a real angel and I don't usually think things like that but that day I did. I couldn't believe this person that I was witnessing was my daughter."

 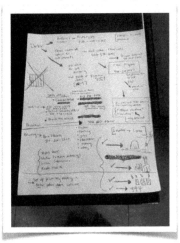

The Decision to Go Back to Jail

Just three weeks after we had met and after we had been spending so much time together flooding Don with all these new experiences, Don made the decision to turn himself in to the police and to end his running once and for all so that we could be together more often and in a safer way. We went to the beach after I drew a whole map of options for Don so he could see all the outcomes visually based on the number of choices he had.

Finally, he was ready that afternoon and together we called Officer Sykes to give her the news. Don wanted to let her know he had met his biological daughter and was ready to stop running from the law and turn himself in.

Don: "Being willing to give up my freedom and walk into a police department was not an easy decision at first, but it came from a sudden realization that in order to keep Cami and become more desirable to her as a human being, I'm going to have to give up a few things. And I knew there were things I was doing in my life that could get me and her in trouble. Once I made this decision, my mind could not be changed. So I made a decision that in order to be able to keep her around, I was going to have to do my time owed in jail. But after we left that gig she brought me to, I went ahead and told her that whenever she was ready we could pack my stuff and drive me to the police station. I emptied my pockets, gave her my chess set, and would enter with only the clothes on my back. And when I did this I never looked back."

Turning Himself In

I was with him that Saturday when he decided for sure to turn himself in, helped him pack, and drove him to the station. For some sort of timing reasons, they couldn't book him in for over three hours, so we had to wait. They actually denied his initial entry and asked him to come back if you can believe that but with his then way of life, a lot can happen in three hours and I knew I should stall time to avoid this. So I got out my Iphone and he and I sat in the police station arm-in-arm on the ground and I streamed the movie *'Good Will Hunting'* for us to pass the time. He loved the movie, as I knew he would. And in fact the movie itself set the tone for the months that were to come. We laughed a lot, disrupting people who would come and go in the police station, but these were our last moments together for a while.

In fact what Don didn't tell me was he was actually risking facing a much longer sentence for having run so many times and it would be up to Judge Kennedy to finally decide. Although jail is never a place you would wish for someone you love to be, I felt better knowing Don would be in jail a while as I prepared myself for what may come next for him upon his release, feeling he would be safer than using on the streets surrounded by gangs. Jail also gave Don an opportunity to process everything that we had experienced together. It was my hope that he could start having a new hope for the future.

It was at that moment that we knew that, one way or another, our next chapter of our lives would have each other in it.

Stop Running and Using for Good

Upon every release prior for most of his life my biological father would run from his probation officer every time he was let out of prison because he couldn't follow the probation regulations that he remain clean: all his drug tests would come back positive. Old habits die hard and stopping is harder but something was different this time. It seemed that the time we spent together during those three weeks reached Don in some way and led him to make the choice on his own to turn himself in to the police and to end his running once and for good. Because after we met, for the first time in his life, Don was willing to try something new: the road to a different kind of freedom.

After asking The Shakespeare Center my neighbor when I lived downtown at the time to borrow their address for a safe return address while he was in jail awaiting a court date for release I also made sure he had this address related to me (even though I actually didn't live there, I lived next door), I knew it would be a good idea for him to have some safe way to keep in contact with me for the next chapter we might share together, whatever that may become. And now that we had a bit more of a definitive release date to plan on, for the next three months, from August to October, Don and I wrote letters back and forth to keep both of us busy.

Another Life

At that time, I was also preparing to travel across the country to bring my car back home to LA from a short stint of time I had spent writing songs and recording a live album with guitarist Guthrie Trapp in Nashville. Every single day on my route back to LA, I made sure to find a post office wherever I was to ensure that letters would be mailed to Don consistently. Sometimes I would write four letters a day, to make sure he had plenty to read. All the while he was writing me back and The Shakespeare Center held onto the letters for me. I did find some irony in the fact that when I used to act quite regularly back in high school, I had landed the role as Viola / Cesario in my only Shakespeare play which was a female character that would disguise herself as a man to protect the person from embarrassment of whom she really loved. I found it interesting and ironic that now later in my real life, once Jenni now calling myself Cami also balancing both worlds of my adoptive and biological self to protect the ones I loved.

The Letters and the Jail Visit

Settled back in LA by the morning I stopped and picked up the letters from Don waiting for me and began to plan a visit.

The Visit in Jail

Don: *"I was sitting on my bunk about one week after I got there to jail when the cop brought me her first letter and I said to myself god damn she really did write. The Pisas on bunk 63 saw that I got a letter and they said "hey white boy who wrote you and what's it say?" So I told them it was my daughter writing me telling me she was gonna come and visit and they said from the way it sounds it sounds like it might be a made up story. A few days later I called out for a visit and so were the pisas who knew I got that letter who got called out for their own visits and they seen her. The second she came in to sit between the glass with me she was wearing a black cape looking thing with bell bottom pants*

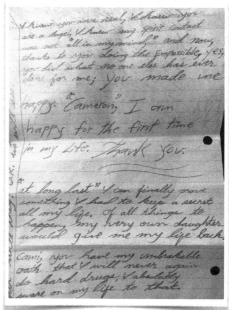

and long black hair down her shoulders and she looked shockingly pretty to the point where all five guys that came to get their own visit that seen her couldn't believe that she was actually my daughter. So when we got back to the dorm, one of the pisas asked permission if he could tell everyone what he had just seen, and asked me "how the hell did you make a chick like that?"

The Hearing

I knew that Don had decided to turn himself in order to keep me in his life, but what he didn't know was I would have stayed in his life somehow and loved him as he was whether he chose that change or not. Maybe somehow he did sense this very thing and maybe that was part of why he did it anyway, just to show me, and perhaps even himself, that he could and would. It was only after he had turned himself in and been released when I discovered that since he had violated his probation so many times - he might have had his probation revoked completely resulting in facing a potential sentence of two to three years - a risk Don secretly was taking just to try and make things right in order for us to get to know one another in a better way. And instead of fear, he chose to have faith just as his gambling nature often led him to have. Don later told me that he had kept this potential sentence and potential grave consequence from me in order to protect me from the pain he thought it might cause me if things didn't go the way he had planned. Fortunately for the both of us we had a bit of luck or perhaps it was compassion or curiosity from others on our side. Could we do the impossible together? Let us wait and see. Upon hearing Don's new plea, the judge decided to give him one more chance and sentenced him to a mere 12 weeks, the standard 90 day sentence for probation violation even though he was well past strike number three, instead of a full 3 years. On the day of Don's court hearing with Judge Kennedy, I woke up earlier than usual with a shortness of breath. I was nervous for him and for the outcome this judge might decide and kept thinking Don's name over and over again. I tried to picture precisely what he might be experiencing at that very minute in time hoping to send him courage and faith that everything would turn out as it was supposed to. I felt like I would be able to protect him in doing this even from afar, which confirmed for me what I had felt shortly after meeting him: that there was a reason for our reconnection, much larger than I could have imagined: I was going to be able to present a bit of safety and protection for him if he chose so as he faced the next part of his life.

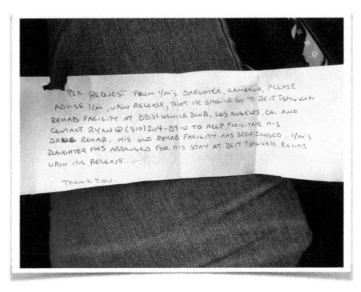

Since this was hearing would determine the outcome so naturally his gamble was much much higher but based on his gambling history for survival he always played to win. He went on that morning to represent himself, sharing the story of having been found by his birth daughter, me, that he was once separated from and pleaded for one more chance because upon our three week reunion and my observations of Don during our time together prior to this, I had began to act as his advocate naturally and shadow him in social situations as a guide based on my experience with this technique with many unique learning students I had worked with before similar to see if it would help redirect thought processes, habits, and behavioral go tos he had. Don presented a strong case and asked for one more chance. The judge miraculously chose to grant Don probation a decision rare to none but I believe the judge looked up our history in the courts system and decided for the uniqueness of our truth to take one more risk with this grant. By all accounts, this was a chance that should have never been granted, but he was being given one more opportunity to follow the probation regulations and maintain a newly found sobriety.

The Release from Jail

A few days before Don was to be released I hadn't received a letter from him yet and I realized that he didn't have any alternative options of where to meet me if our plan to meet outside of the jail exit doors failed to work. I started to imagine the possibilities of all that could go wrong so I phoned up the sheriff and asked to be patched into the main jail officer to prepared inmates release jacket to send Don a message. Now everyone who's ever known someone who has done time knows that jails and prisons do not take messages for inmates but I was desperate to make sure our meeting upon his release would work or that he would have an alternative meeting spot to find me just in case it didn't otherwise I knew for certain based on my studies of the human condition that old habits would certainly step in.

When the sheriff finally patched me through it took some convincing of the officer that answer my call, but finally when I told our biological reunion story that by writing this note with exactly where I would be waiting with an alternative location listed if he couldn't find me as well in his release jacket, that he had an opportunity to save a life, he hand wrote the message and placed it in there for me, I'll always remember him so.

On the morning of Oct 5th, I got to the downtown men's correctional facility as early as I could since I myself didn't know exactly when they would let him go or which street he would be released to and began waiting for him at 6am across the street from downtown LA county jail. I made sure to look at every man passing by hoping I'd see my birth father when he was released. And at exactly 7:03 I saw him walk out of the door and cross the opposite street. I screamed, "Don! several times to make sure he saw me and when he did, he changed his direction towards me after three long months we embraced and our first safe day together began.

CHAPTER 6
HOPE

From the moment of my birth father's release from jail, we began doing as many memorable activities together as I could think of. We started with ...

Adventures of Assimilation
From the moment of my birth father's release from jail, we began doing as many memorable activities together as I could think of. We started with trips to Alcoholics Anonymous meetings where he could listen to stories and speak about his with me as support by his side and a visit to the self realization center.

Our first adventure was to the Cuban cafe for a cup of the strongest coffee and to stop into an AA meeting there. I remembered upon my DUI the signature time cards they had to sign so I started a page especially for Don. He loved speaking and sharing his story with me listening there, even though we weren't absolutist for the AA program, rather we were moderationalistds with me leading the amounts and timings of each experience to test out aiding in the management of usage before total abstinence since he was more of a chooser abuser of alcohol much more than a lost user and how to provide the support and attention he craved. Then we drove out to the self realization center for our first real moment together in what was to become Don's new life. At this time, I also started to organize the first of a paper trail process I ultimately designed for his future court date, creating a green folder of paperwork that I would later call *Don's Reverse Olson file*. We also returned to the library where I even showed Don how to make a resume.

Creative Solution Solving Suggestions

We were also in search of a recovery home where Don could stay for a while so he would have an address and program required by court. But over time as I took him to different sober living house environments and obtained resources for homeless people, many had specific extra requirements if an applicant seemed to fall into a category with mental health challenges by their standards and these demands were scary and of no interest to Don. After observing Don for these next weeks I concluded that he had formulated defense mechanisms to protect himself for survival rather than truly having a mental illness as the prisons who institutionalized for him for his repetitive behaviors as an underprivileged child conditioned him to think, something he would of never thought he was doing. I also came to understand that he was a drug user by choice and his relationship to using was his choice the same as it was his choice when upon finally meeting me, it was his choice to stop. It was at this point when I realized creative solution solving systems would offer him exposure to a world and interactions he never had as a way to slowly assimilate him into society, and if he wanted to, into my life.

Untented Temporary Times

In the meantime, I had to figure out where he would sleep temporarily, and how he would live as it was way too soon at the time for me to have even considered him staying with me and what was later to transpire. So the first I did was think of all the homeless hideouts Don had described to me and shown me and created a similar styled homeless space for him going to the neighbors of my then downtown LA flat I was still living in for a short time longer, and intentionally created an area of assimilation that was almost a mere replica of Don's previous encampments for us to discover together unbeknownst to him. I had it approved and securely tucked away where there was nowhere for him to go when I left him to sleep at night and arrived back early each next day to get him each and every morning. He was stashed away on the ledge of a hidden hillside a less than block from my home. I didn't want it to be too comfortable for him so he only had a few things supplied, all the while letting him keep the impression that we had found these things by chance. All he had then was a mattress, a pillow, a few blankets, and some clothes, besides access to his things we had packed together prior to turning himself in that I had stored close by for him and a small laminated water proof note with his description and my contact that I had made for him to carry for emergencies.

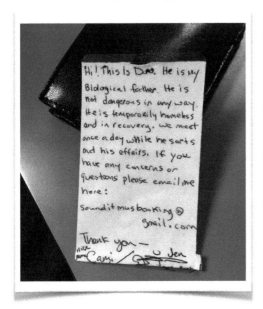

Family Fun Field Trip Adventures Deluxe

During this window of almost four weeks, we weathered the rain and kept adventure at our feet. We went horseback riding, boating, and hiking as part of our early day local 'family fun adventures'. I would continue to blindfold him into my home so he could not see, and we would cook, and, and watch movies, in the event that I might need to protect in case he might change back to his old ways. To my surprise he kept following my lead, moving forward towards a new life day after day. He had his first Halloween in West Hollywood, his first frozen yogurt, his first In and Out Burger, a clean shower and a shave, with hot meals each day. From burritos to Chinese, to sushi and Thai, we tried everything together, exploring ways to engage with the world in more productive and positive ways.

The first stage of this was exploring Don's options to become more self-reliant and how he could obtain a small bit of money each month in safer ways to be able to manage his needs and take care of himself. Baby steps forward together towards this large feat.

Music and Chess, he liked to play best

Don was a great musician early upon receiving his first electric guitar, a Tesco from Kmart. A self taught musician, the skill of playing music would protect him for the rest of his life. He also developed a love for chess at a really young age and his skills were extraordinary. He would also teach himself this mostly when he was alone learning the winning games from all the greats in books that he had found in the library of David R McMillan boys home, playing those very greats in his mind with those books even until this

day. This too, would be a skill embedded in talent that would save his life, more than once, from the troubled outside so both of these tools became very interracial parts of our days together both so he could keep a part of his identity and past alongside him as he transitioned with me into this new way of life and so he could bring with him his own set of skills and passions to show me.

And I shared with him my life in music, my art, and the baby pictures I had kept from my foster and adoptive home.

The Good Spirits that Guide

One of his most admirable coping mechanisms that I picked up on early on was when he would talk out loud to his 'spirit friends' that he later told me that he made when he was a child quite regularly when left in his own safe space, even if just a few feet away. He also definitely knew the difference between fantasy and truth but these spirit friends would protect him as he processed things in his life from being mostly outside in his youth or otherwise locked up in prison for most of his life. It seemed to me that these spirit friends were there with him to help him work things out with himself and between himself and the world. It was my perspective that he wasn't a danger to himself nor I and

so I warmly welcomed all of him. Sometimes he would even rock himself back and forth as well when deep in thought so as to comfort himself or simply to relax. Noting these things about him gave me flashes of my own childhood self. After having arrived at the Alpert's, when I played with dolls to work things out or have fun, I I too would speak out loud to myself and rocked myself to bed every night until I was twelve. Apples don't fall far from their trees.

Late in The Evenings

Late in the evenings we would talk for hours under the stars at the partial encampment I created near my then apartment in downtown LA right after Don was released from jail as a familiar yet safe step towards assimilation. Often we would share stories with one another about our lives and our thoughts on genetic DNA memory from possible lifetimes ago. We both shared similar sentiments of times reminiscent of the 1600's in and about England, he a knight, me a queen. We would laugh at our shared bond and then sit in silence breathing

111

up the cold winter air. One night while we were spending time getting to know each other in my car because of how cold it was, I drove us to a dead end street so we could sit in the warmth of my car and share more stories. It felt so safe and so comfortable there with him, that I fell asleep on Don's lap in the backseat only to be startled and woken up by the cops pulling up to see what we were doing illegally parked in a cul de sac downtown. I instantly jumped out of the car waving my hands up in the air saying it's not what it looks like, I'm not a prostitute, this is my biological father, we were recently reunited..... while Don sat on a nearby curb to stay out of the way of any interaction with the cops, yet quietly chuckling to himself about my reaction. I had been so nervous to see cops, but he was used to this and more calm than I. They took our IDs and checked out our backgrounds while Don, now on probation just having been released a few days prior, sat patiently on the sidewalk waiting to be taken. Yet, it seemed there were notes in their computers as to who we were and after some questioning, they simply let us go.

Social Services Support

Shortly thereafter we went to the Compton Social Services Building, I as slid into role as his advocate and social skills shadow along with being his biological daughter by now, and was able to secure his first general relief package supporting those out of work (GR) or who can't work with an EBT card that also included monthly food stamps so he had access to food, learning as I went.

For months I would drive us down to Compton and wait in the lines with him, shadowing him to fill out each packet properly, guiding him as he turned them in. The process to obtain social services was even hard for me to keep up with. Simply dialing in the numbers took a lot of focus and a very long time to get it all right. Imagine if you were hungry and homeless and high.

112

Health and A Real Doctor

Now that we established food stamps and obtained General Relief (GR) I budgeted his pennies for him managing his life with $197 cash each month and $225 in food stamps to get him the bare minimum without hardly ever coming out of pocket to keep both of us self reliant guiding him towards independence. Since Don never had a bank account and didn't feel comfortable inside of them, I simply created a portable safe for that and held it all for him. We also got Don medical reinstated so he could get regular health check ups but it soon became clear that he never had a legitimate patient doctor relationship so the next thing we did was secure a primary care doctor through medical and shadowed him through every appointment as well so he couldn't ask the staff for anything.

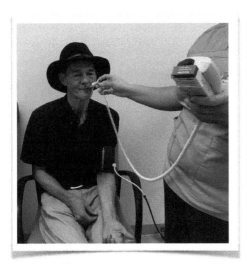 

In the beginning I watched him like a hawk, redirecting and steering him towards safer choices to keep our path on track. Finally a real prescription for an inhaler for asthma that he really did need was legitimately his. It was at this time I realized that he had never had a trusted doctor that listened to his needs at the same time he never had been on a doctor visit honestly. This was also the start of the medical paper trail Don needed for SSI application and more long term security later down the line.

Hope of the Valley

We discovered Hope of the Valley truly by chance through the AA meeting book one day while I had been searching for a new one for Don to attend while I was planning on running some errands nearby.

Turns out this one hour stop turned out to be one of the best and most fortunate stops we made. There, Don not only got an hour in for the AA meetings I was initiating he attended for the court, but he also got to shower, some used clothes, a hot lunch, and ultimately an amazing set of resources that they later gave us upon our return. We also were pointed into the direction of where to get for free meals daily for Don as well as free groceries which really helped in the early stages of budgeting since Don didn't have much

and my goal and role was to shadow him towards self reliance not save and take care of him. Sometimes the groceries would be old with bugs so eventually we stopped picking up bags at other places but never did this happen at Hope of the Valley, they always made sure to provide hot lunches and resources daily, and it truly was this amazing place. Almost instantly we met Laurie Craft, the Chief Program Officer there. She helped us get Don into a transitional sober living bed at a facility in north Hollywood after we had visited a more rigid one

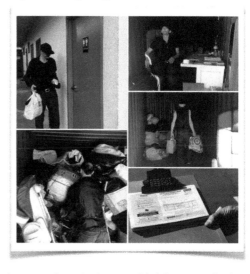

that required too many mental health check ups and meds that wouldn't have worked well for Don. We were on the search to secure something for the judge since he didn't end up getting into Beit T'shuvah based on what their program provided there and at this time though I had started to transition him into the inside where I was now staying in Studio City and was still blind folding Don for the same protective reasons as before, so he couldn't come and go as he chose, but also had the freedom to turn about face and return to his old life with drugs If he ever so chose to, no hard feelings keeping my life with him in still separate and safe. Laurie was an incredible help.

In our search for a safe living space for Don before we decided that it was best and easiest to stay with me, we checked out a place called Stone which didn't resonate with Don because it was more of a mental health sober living space with lots of regiments and rules. It was about this time that Laurie from Hope of the Valley offered to introduce us to Gino the head of a sober transitional home for men in Burbank to see if this was a compatible spot for Don. We met G at a nearby Starbucks in Burbank and jumped into his 4X4 truck to visit the space nearby to which Don seemed comfortable enough in at the

HOPE OF THE VALLEY
RESCUE MISSION

October 20, 2016

To Whom It May Concern:

I had the pleasure of meeting with Mr. Don Logsdon today to discuss various programs that Hope of the Valley Rescue Mission offers that would potentially be a good fit for Mr. Longsdon. We took the time to walk through what his needs are, and which programs would be the most beneficial for him at this point in his life.

Mr. Logsdon is very eager to find a comprehensive program that will give him the utmost opportunity for personal growth, as well as recovery, and is willing to do whatever it takes and put forth the effort to make this come to pass.

If you should have any questions, please do not hesitate to contact me.

Sincerely,

Laurie Craft

Laurie Craft, Site Director, Help Center
laurie@hopeofthevalley.org
w 818-804-5508 c-818-322-2644

beginning. They had group meetings once a week, rotating chores for the shared communal space, and most of the men paid something for a bed. Since we had only just started Don on GR (General Relief) support and food stamps at the time, he had about $197 cash relief a month and $206 for food stamps. I managed his needs and necessities with that and donations for over two years before upgrading him to SSI at the end of the third year. Once Don approved it he men's transitional home, we moved him out of the selected bushes that was a transitional space towards indoors living, had him stay with me for a few weeks while we set up his next transition nearby my then condo, and proceeded to check Don into

Hope of the Valley's Men's home in Burbank which ended up being close to a two month stay before we realized ultimately he was better off with me, all or nothing.

Yet, it was the best option to try out the transitional home to obtain an address for the judge and with that we set up an agreement where every Friday Don would volunteer at one of Hope of the Valley's donation centers in exchange for his bed. The night before he was to move in, I went to the store, got a few plastic bins, filled them up with toiletries, packed his clothes, and gathered blankets for his bed.

Each day I would be there at 8am to take him around and about to different activities and appointments and each night just before they locked the doors shut I would drop him off to rest to see how things would go for him. It didn't take long for him to decide, however, to fully stick with me. Though the beds cost $500 each, Don essentially had no money so I negotiated that I would shadow him at one of the Hope of the Valley donation collection sites for him to earn his space.

Often I would shadow him there to make sure the responsibilities would get done and other times I would stay close by and see what he could do alone. Most of the time he did better with me there so to keep him busy and focused when donations weren't being signed in, we would play chess and cards and read together. One slow day Don even welcome my encouragement for him to write apology letters to anyone he thought he may have hurt even if it was just a mere exercise. These too were included in his reverse Olson

file I was making of Don's transformation for the judge to see. It would be during this period that I got a good idea of where Don's independence would shine most.

But the sober living home began to get rough and became scary for Don there and one morning he figured out a bus route with the help of one of the other residents there despite my requests to not discuss things like that for his protection, and he ran away. This was an extremely scary moment for me because now anything could happen to Don and this also confirmed the reality, the common assumption of what would happen, that old habits won't ever die and that drugs and Don's old life would eventually win him over. But

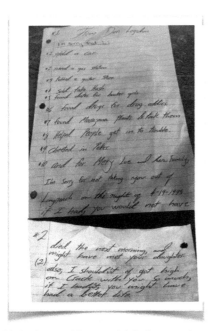

I didn't give up, I just couldn't. I spent the whole searching to find him starting with visiting the emergency meet locations we set up together at the start of this journey for the just in case moments, just like this. See Don didn't use phones and wasn't really up on technology. Phones and computers were such a challenge for him and simply took too long so planning ahead considering his methods of thinking was something I constantly did by this time. My heart was in panic though, and I went to every single spot we had ever been to. Twice. I searched until nightfall and absolutely did not give up until I found him to make sure this was the choice he'd really want to make after how far we had gotten by this point. I just wanted to look him in the eyes and softly ask him for certain if returning to running was really the life he wanted or if perhaps we could together negotiate and create a new life that felt right for him. Finally, literally a shadow step behind him the whole day, I found him around ten pm that night, drunk and sleeping outside on the door stoop of the dwelling where he used to frequent. One step forward, two steps back. Luckily, I found him in time before the cops did as he was still very much on probation and heavily watched even if at a distance because of me, but I had the chance I wanted to give him the option to keep running or return blind folded back with me. Probation officers don't care about if you made a mistake, they care about the safety of others, they care about the law. And when on probation, especially when on Ab109 both drugs and drinking are simply not allowed. But I knew with parameters of regulation and a new system full of love there was a chance that Don could have a life he had never before dreamed of. This was the turning point for me as well. I knew if he was to see real transformation it would only be by us being together and it was an all or nothing moment. I realized in that minute that either he was to come with as his advocate and shadow or nothing at all. It didn't take me but three minutes to decide.

Probation

Don was put on probation for a year, the standard length for drug and absconding charges and consistency and following protocol is really all that matters.

But it is not easy. You have to know the schedule, know the location of every appointment, you have to receive your mail. You have to keep organized, and socialized, and motivated to not fail - which is nearly impossible for most offenders, especially those of Don's kind. Don's weekly probation meetings and testing converted to monthly since I was now in the picture as his advocate and social skills shadow.

Upon Don's initial release, it was first Officer L who helped us through the process with phone calls and emails to figure out the next steps for Don would be and informed me of his new assigned probation officer Mrs Officer B. I started advocating on Don's behalf, emailing to scheduling these meetings for him, then each month I got him ready, drove him there, and shadowed him socially inside the police station sitting with him all the way through each one so I could help him complete each step of this and to know all the risks if he were to make more mistakes.

Why those officers let me do this, I am not fully sure, but I am so grateful that they did. And I do believe that every offender who may need an advocate and a social skills and processing shadow to help complete requirements like these would be a really positive program to devise and implement one day for special cases. Those two officers went an extra mile to communicate back with me on Don's behalf and let me do what J did. And Officer B was really a Godsend if there ever was one because she allowed me ample

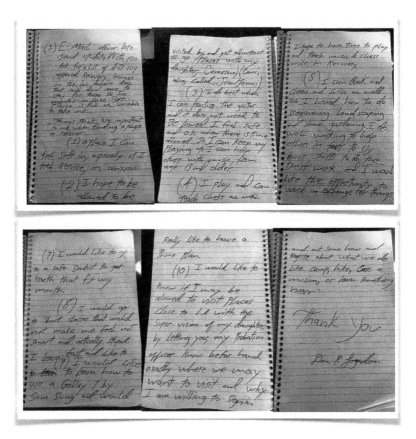

freedom to guide Don and help him in my own creative solution solving ways through this whole process for a whole year, something never been done before.

Daily then weekly I emailed details and photos to kept her informed of our whereabouts and activities, of his progress and perspective, and all the good things he'd done. She even eventually honored the Jewish custom we shared with Shabbat letting me give him small bouts of wine in measurements for him to feel still as himself and later allowed a medical marijuana card when it became legal so there was no pressure for psych meds or to be totally dry as long as I measured and managed the supply at the proper times. It was all in the parameters of the delivery and framing that worked for us. I knew it wouldn't work for everyone, most drug addicts go back and that is a fact. But Don defied the norm in his own ways just as I did. Don also learned all about my Jewish side of life, learned all of the music for the Shabbat Services I occasionally lead and joined me weekly for a long time as we were even given a residency at what Don would call *Temple Beth* in Highland Park. I'll always be forever grateful to that board for letting us do this, as sharing in the culture, music, customs, and holidays became a huge part of our bond.

His probation officer also also eventually granted us passes to go camping so I could show Don what real camping was like to assimilate him more into society's light. We also visit Santa Barbara, San Francisco, Big Sur, Santa Rosa, and Humboldt, eventually picking up a small travel trailer offered to Don at a quaint sweet RV park up there by a special person named Butch so he would always have access to a roof over his head, though by now even still blindfolded, he was living with me.

We called it Safe Space Don's Place on wheels.

And while yes, abuse of power may be a legitimate concern within certain police stations, jails, and prisons around the country in the police force, these officers to me never instigated those thoughts to cross my mind, rather theses very Officers represent what good cops are. They too are up against so much particular to their situations themselves while working to make this world a safer straighter place, their lives on the line, and

personally I am forever grateful to every single one of them for the chance they took on us, for what they did for Don, and for what they did for me.

Creative Solution Solving

As I began to integrate and assimilate Don into my daily life those second and third set of months I also moved back to the valley in a condo I had and brought Don and the blindfold concept with me. In order to balance my own life separate from his, my jobs, my friends, my

family and such, all the while Don's preference for the outdoors prevailed as well as leaving Don at all my home unsupervised was not an option I chose until years later when trust and routine was deeply established and embedded. I sought out far away protected secluded parks where there were no ways to leave or wander about near my appointments where I would leave Don for a few hours at a time. I called these areas that subtly mimicked how he used to live, a temporary *safe space Don's place* while I would go and handle my responsibilities.

I would pack him a lunch, coffee, candy to go, and a cigar of course as two a way was the agreed upon limit, and a backpack with chess, a radio, books, and some games and often even a box with his music equipment. Once it became legal, he was also granted a medical marijuana card which was really helpful for his anxiety and comfort level so we worked together for weeks to process the difference between medical and recreational behaviors and agreed also never to talk to or take anything from strangers to keep him as protected and thoughtful as possible. It may sound a bit juvenile but really it was important discussions to have to devise parameters together in both of our best interests as partners, and most of the time, Don went along. We did many things in the early days to support the process of him

121

getting through and getting off of probation. I also made sure to bring Don to visit with my birth uncle Jimmy from time to time to keep their relationship going.

As time went on we were comfortable with tailoring each decision about things specifically to Don's case and relationship to using or alcohol so he still could maintain his own ideas and feelings about things while shifting his relationship to them. For example, in his perspective about hard drugs using was that for the most part he chose and managed his choices intentionally. With the exception of heroin and some of the more heavy physically addictive drugs, for the most part he would choose when he did and didn't want to use or drink and so when he met me it was just another choice to make. In my personal option, for Don specifically, measured moderation came with a reason and purpose to choose to do and once we started to work together he allowed me to manage that with him, but we both knew this dynamic we built was extremely unique to us. For example, there are a lot great themes and insights in approaches to behavioral modification from AA that are good to take always, but there ended up being deeper reasons why lot that didn't end up applying to us so we took what worked. Turns

out when processing situations on a case by case basis there is a spectrum for almost everything. It was really amazing to discover and see Don transform of his own volition over the years and more amazing at the fact that he would listen to me.

To my surprise and eternal gratefulness, his probation officer perceived many of these approaches in observation as positive and allowed me to guide Don within these parameters at arms length distance sense of freedom and I think she allowed for this as she watched the impossible unfold in our partnership together. Thanks to her we both were granted a second chance at life together.

Released From The System For The First Time

After two court hearings bookending about ten months of probation meetings, eventually, Don was released from the probation department and Judge K had me stand in the courtroom to honor our feat.

ON FEBRUARY 9, 2017, THE PROBATION OFFICER INITIATED A REFERRAL TO THE
HEALTHRIGHT360 SYSTEM NAVAGATION SERVICES TO START HELPING THE PSP G
SECURITY. HE HAS ALSO BEEN ESCORTED BY HIS DAUGHTER TO THE DOCTORS F
AND HAS RECEIVED A CLEAN BILL OF HEALTH.

POSTRELEASED SUPERVISED PERSON'S STATEMENT:

ON MARCH 30, 2017, THE PSP WAS ASKED ABOUT HIS PARTICIPATION AT THE "HO
ALLEY RESCUE MISSION", HE REPLIED, "YES, I AM STILL VISITING ONLY AT THIS '
M VOLUNTEERING MYSELF AS A SPEAKER AND MUSICIAN WITH MY DAUGHTER '
E RATHER THAN USING THEM FOR SERVICES FOR MYSELF BECAUSE I AM BE
F RELIANT WITH THE HELP OF MY DAUGHTER. I PREFER BEING WITH MY DAI

LIVING STANDARDS OF SOCIETY, AND SHE SHOWS ME DIFFERENT THINGS I
EXPERIENCED. BECAUSE OF OUR BOND, I PREFER TO SPEND MY TIME WITH
INTEREST IN HARD DRUGS OR CRIME. I HAVE NEVER HAD SUCH HELP OR SI
I WANT TO CONTINUE THIS WAY OF LIFE WITH HER."

EVALUATION:

THE PSP CONTINUES TO REMAIN IN COMPLIANCE WITH THE TERMS AND CO
RELEASE COMMUNITY SUPERVISION. HE IS REPORTING AS REQUIRED AND

It was pretty special and a day I won't forget, and I will forever appreciate him for all he did for us too.

Towards the end of Don's probation term he started to really show transformative signs not only in his actions and attitude but also in his look. He had lost several years from his old haggard look and started to take up a new healthy look at his real age of 56. Officer B told me of a program at UCLA in the Dental School where the students there would work on people's teeth for credit and since Don didn't have any, he ended up being the first homeless person to get dentures from their program. We went every Thursday for ten weeks and spent time with the students so he could get some teeth. Eventually, though, he would hold them in his pocket saying they were almost too nice to wear.

From Vagrant to Volunteer

By this time, we started to do more volunteer work with a focus for various non profits. This was to pivot Don's position from living street life to giving and leading instead. We started volunteering for Hope of The Valley's lunch times and attended their annual Thanksgiving lunch on our first thanksgiving together, eventually graduating to becoming one of the featured fundraiser entertainers three years later. Around that same time I also brought Don

into a foster group home that I had programmed for creating a songwriting and recording workshop for the youth there. This time around Don joined me as a specialist on my team helping them make a song and cd which was the start of his transformation towards becoming a volunteer and soon after, a speaker performer himself. Together we began creating short music dinner performances for Recycled Resources for the Homeless that offered evening meals and a place inside a church for those experiencing homelessness to sleep also located down the street from Temple Beth Israel where we would often lead a reform style musical Shabbat service together on Friday Nights for their community. It was really special to see the reactions and connections from those experiencing homelessness there when Don shared his part of our story and perspectives.

We also played a lot of our own music together, performed regularly at local venues, and attended music concerts.

These early experiences became the pilot experiments and first of many music with story and songs programs we devised together called *Home is Where the Heart is, An Adoption and Biological Reunion Story Program* to share our reunion and transformation with story and song to reach those experiencing homelessness, incarceration, addiction issues, foster care adoption and birth reunions, or any other relatable hardships as well to encourage others to have the courage to try something creative and new as well.

And because of our deep connection with music which we had fostered by playing music and performing together, Don continued to join me for the programs we would create for Hope of the Valley's new homes for families where we volunteered to assist the children in learning about music and songs. Not surprisingly, they loved him too.

Stability

Throughout the next year we would graduate to a new level of stability for Don. He was able to get reading glasses from my brother Matt who is an optometrist, obtain a mailing address, update his ID to the new California ID, secure SSI, get a regular prescription for ensure and any other meds he needed, completely clear of Hep B and C that he had been exposed to while in prison, created a special savings account for Don and health directives to protect his future, and stabilize his meals, locating him as close to me as possible, my new home, without actually making him a legal resident so he could keep his homeless status just in case he wanted to go, rescued some animals, and never missed a holiday or birthday.

We were incredibly lucky to have one another and the support of everyone around us.

(my mom who adopted me meeting my birth father for the first time. She would continue to welcome him into all our family holiday events.)

Or perhaps it was simply just fate. And all on his own Don began to transform.

CHAPTER 7
HOME IS WHERE THE HEART IS

Over the course of four more years, our personal dynamic got closer forming an even stronger bond of togetherness as a team, his self proclaimed transformation and my new sense of center remarkable. Don and I began to grow our partnership outward to offer…

A Labor of Love

Over the course of four more years, our personal dynamic got closer forming an even stronger bond of togetherness as a team, his self proclaimed transformation and my new sense of center remarkable. Don and I began to grow our partnership outward to offer support and motivation to others promoting healing change with creative solution solving. As our journey continued to unfold in the months passing by, I watched the people around me suffer in sinking

partnerships, not feeling heard and not feeling a sense of home that was starved for so often and from all that I discovered in meeting my birth father, I wanted to share a piece of what this unconventional unconditional love that Don and I had discovered was. Never once did we desperately seek a need from one another, rather we merely mutually showed up to present and provide and were nothing other than transparently and honestly ourselves with one another mutually providing and sharing what we had and who we are with one another in a symbiotic common goal of. And it was simply in being fully present each day with both ourselves and with one another that made our balanced relationship work so right. One thing I learned most through this profound biological reunion on the journey to finding me inside my adopted self, is that sometimes in the storm of all the fighting - it's more often to be heard through the thunder less than to always be captain of the ship, and in the end what really matters is if we as individuals face and fix ourselves ultimately, this leads to finding and feeling that deepest sense of safety and home.

Documenting the Moments, *Homeless: The Soundtrack*

As far back as I can remember, a part of me always loved documenting the present in some way to preserve as many moments as possible to make sure they are never forgotten. Instinctually from the very beginning of our biological reunion I was driven to find as many ways to document all the stages in one form or another whether it be photos, short video clips, or journaling to somehow imprint this amazing experience I was having forever. It didn't occur to me that there might be something extraordinarily special about our story until someone else started to pay close attention to our unique partnership develop and Don transform in our journey.

One night by chance at a dinner party back during the early few months right when Don had just started to serve his time in jail and we were in our letter writing phase, I met the influential professional, of the several we would eventually meet, that expressed interest in sharing our story and it's value. When I first saw him I could have sworn I recognized him as his disheveled look reflected that of someone slightly homeless so I thought maybe I had met him before while out on the street. Making me think of Don, I introduced myself and started to share the story of finding my biological father and sharing our pictures with him as this was all freshly on my mind. As it would turn out he wasn't homeless as all, in fact Steve Schwartz and his wife Paula Mae worked on films, felt there was a special story in ours, and connected us with a documentary director who ended up spending a few months on and off with us starting a few weeks after Don got out to capture bits and pieces of our reunion story as a labor of love. At the time I had no idea she was Irene Taylor Brodsky, the Peabody Award winning established director, I just knew her as Irene and her team interviewing us and following us through the next phase of our journey capturing it scene by scene. Later she stated that it was one of the more grueling filming experiences in her career at the time being out there on the street with us due to the long hours and how many things we did together throughout each day but she hung in there and *Homeless: the Soundtrack* the short documentary was born.

It was really hard at first to film because I felt responsible for Don and his process and wanted to stay aware and focused on him and his safety and well-being being the priority especially early on while his transitions and newly found sobriety from hard narcotics and tie life he lived out there were just beginning as was the relationship with me. To be thoughtful, protective, open, and spontaneous all at the same time was a daily balance but I was able to trust my inner guide and take lead from Don as he really loved filming the short doc too.

To this day we are so thankful and grateful at the opportunity we had to spend with Irene and her team and that footage of memories is forever cherished.

Filming for the First Time

It was actually during our first weeks together we were noticed by a young director of photography, Justin Cornell, as we were eating Chinese fast food on the ground in a parking lot. Perhaps it was the dichotomy of our difference that sparked his interest, or perhaps the connection we had starting from even early on that emanated outward every time we were together. Whatever it was that drew him in when he approached us to ask if he could spend a day or two interviewing and following us around Don perked up at the idea and it seemed a neat idea to me.

Since I always had an admiration and drive to document moments for the memory of them myself, it seemed more than chance that now here was a talented eye willing to join and capture us from his lens and that was inspiring. And it was his early footage catching our earliest

133

days together and Don's pivotal process of deciding to turn himself in on camera and our photos of those days together that ultimately helped me piece together our story to share this exciting new journey to the producer that I happened to meet those few weeks later.

Manhattan, Tribeca Film Festival

Homeless: the Soundtrack developed into a short documentary capturing nuggets and raw moments between Don and I as our biological journey, our musical bond, and his transformation that began to take place while we were together. And the documentary began to open many doors of opportunity for us to share our story with more people as it began to screen in the festival circuit. We were even invited to attend, perform, and speak at *Tribeca Film Festival* in Manhattan, fulfilling Don's lifelong dream to one day go to New York. For two weeks with the support of the Schwartz', the film team, and some good friends, Don was able to have several amazing nights out on the town and a few first time memorable music experiences in his life. Prior to going out East, I made sure to research all the state laws and regulations as well as all the local police stations and hospitals in order to avoid any possibility issue or incident since smoking and out of state medical marijuana cards weren't acceptable there and our dynamic was still pretty new, and secured us a private flat with a kitchen so I could manage his routine there. Using creative measures to keep Don safe and legal while feeling good and focused felt perfectly applicable for such a special yet important trip. I dispensed small measurements of Patron Coffee XO and nicotine patches became the alternative and to my surprise Don did extremely well. We attended screenings and q & a for the film, saw old friends and city monuments, and performed at several venues from my old stomping ground New York days when I used to hub out of there almost yearly to perform and write music myself.

We performed at The Bitter End, The Sidewalk Cafe, and Rockwood Music Hall in addition to performing at the festival and Don even got to play one of the great local players and win a game of chess. Aligning my past to share it in the present with my birth father was extremely profound, like everything I ever did in my life was leading up to these unforgettable moments. It was also truly amazing to me all the support that came out of the woodwork for Don and I, the music relationships I had built over the years as an independent musician all stepped forward with support from Gibson, Daddario, Guitar Center, and Bose, lending us gear and pitching in to contribute something for our experience there which was really special for me.

What was especially touching was Sharon who ran a huge portion of the film festival and the Tribeca staff connecting and showing so much such support for Don. I valued so much that it was largely due to her that we were invited to the *Tribeca Film Festival* personally granting Don an opportunity to experience his dream of going to New York in the first place.

Homeless: the Soundtrack even ended up winning an honorable mention award as well.

First Time for Don Recording in a Professional Studio

Right before that trip to New York I decided to bring Don to a professional recording studio for his first time to have him guest on a song of mine.

We ended up recording an EP together live with a full band lead and produced by Drew Taubenfeld with Erik Kertes on bass, Rob Humphrys on drums, and Will Herrington on keys as a favor and ultimately featured Don's own style of playing in the form of a jam. Don then met my close friend Eric Boulanger, owner of Bakery Mastering who I knew since he started working with Doug Sax in Mastering at the Mastering Lab in Ojai many years before. Throughout most of my independent recording career, Eric had mastered some sometimes mixed almost

all of my music albums to date and so when he was open to mastering our little EP for us as well, I jumped at scheduling the chance. Because of Eric, Don got to hear his performance in the mastering studio on the big mastering studio speakers as well and that blew him away. EEric also gave us our very own pressed vinyl version.

We manufactured that recording along with an interview with Don to CD with my long-time CD manufacturer Harout from Hollywood discs, and we did a photoshoot with my friend and photographer Jeff Fasano while he was out in LA and prepared to share our recording. It was just so neat to weave Don this deep into my life.

Up the West Coast

Later that year, a few months after the Tribeca Film Festival, the documentary was doing well in the film festival circuit in the short doc category and the director Irene invited Don and I to perform at her house in Portland in preparations for possible future screenings and performances together. So I packed all our stuff into our travel trailer and headed up the West Coast replicating my old indie tour route I used to do back in the day for Don to experience with me. He even ate clams for the first time while we were on the

coast and he visited the Jimi Hendrix museum and played electric guitar right outside of it when we reached Seattle. In between all of our coastal adventures, we made the stop at the directors house in Portland for a private screening of the film, Q and A, and live performance for her colleagues and closest friends.

Up On the Big Screen

Upon returning to LA the short doc had a short run at the Laemmle Theaters as well which was really cool to have friends and family attend and see the film on the big screen. Friends and family came out for that and we were extremely touched by their response and the film's impact.

RMWF and Colorado Springs Rescue Mission

Later that year we were also invited to go to Colorado Springs as performing guests of the Rocky Mountain Women's Festival when they screened *Homeless: the Soundtrack* and then we performed and spoke at the Colorado Springs Homeless Rescue Mission and Don saw his first real snow. He began to process other people's experiences experiencing homelessness a bit differently there when he saw some folks sitting out in such cold. He said a lot of inspirational things making sure his audience knew he wasn't there to convert anyone or turn them away from being homeless rather he said he wasn't against

any of it but that if they could hook up with someone they trusted sometime like how he did with his daughter sometimes the right partner can lead the way to a safer and warmer day. It was never about better, it simply was about alternatives.

Though we had volunteered in LA with several centers and regularly now at Hope of the Valley we had ideas to develop a clearer delivery of our story and message. I was so proud of his profoundness and great skill at speaking that day that it inspired me hone in on a performance program we had started to design together that we were calling *Home is Where the Heart is Program with Cami and Don* the Biological *Duo* where we shared our reunion and transformation journey through story and song. What started out as a 45 minute event first hosted by a college of mine at a temple touching on themes

Home is Where My Heart Is A Biological Reunion

of homelessness and addiction, adoption, biological reunions, and family, and our story in between and it was moderate by a college friend of mine Mayim who was experienced at leading these sorts of things. It was a memorable and special evening.

We set up a table with all of the artifacts displaying our lives and reunion story. Mayim moderated the event with us and Don performed and spoke especially well. Ultimately, this event took place because of Mayim's initial invitation to have Don and I write about our biological reunion story for her online blog on Groknation, which they published offering us an even larger platform to share our story. The article along with our previous performance programs inspired the second generation of a more developed event called Home is Where the Heart is, with story and song performance program. And in fact, Mayim had become the first person to successfully employ Don, allowing me to have him write his version of our story for her blog with me, which led to writing this memoir. She was always so good to Don.

Screenings and Performances

From there we added to our volunteering and began performing and speaking for other events and programs as well as at the Malibu Film Society where the Schwartz family belonged to screen the film and perform and talk about new ways to approach solving homelessness in the neighboring areas. Around this time we were also beginning to cross paths again with foster youth aiding them in writing and recording songs as a part of their identity building experiences again and it was really great to see Don step up into a leader teacher role model position with them.

Celia Center, Adoptee Voices, and meeting Jeanette Yoffe

As we were balancing performing, speaking, volunteering, and teaching,I got an email from a close maternal birth cousin of mine introducing me to a non profit called Celia Center founded by a fellow fostered adoptee who also had been in biological reunion who was hosting an arts festival called adoptee voices and that I should really submit something for it. I barely made the submission cut off date but she welcomed me to play the piano in the lobby during the art exhibit portion and then had me sing heaven to all of the guests while Don sat with me. It was such an incredible night. What is even more special about Jeanette Yoffe is her compassion, intuitiveness, and leadership ability to bring so many people together in a safe space. In the journey of her life as an actress in New York, she eventually moved to LA, Changed

gears, became a therapist, a speaker, and mom, and built Celia Center named after her birth mother to aid all members of the constellation in healing and growth offering support groups, educational seminars, annual conferences, and monthly programs including other current or former fostered, adoptees, those in reunion, those still in search, and those deep in turmoil still working things out, also birth mothers and birth family members were invited to attend as well as adoptive families, social workers, and budding therapists interested in this particular field of focus and the work she does bringing support all members of the adoption constellation is incredible.

Through Jeanette and her programming we visited and performed at Wolf Connection, we were invited to speak and perform at the CUB (Concerned United Birthparents Annual Retreat), and I began working closely with her as her social media maven maiden as she prepared to host the National Adoption Conference the following year where we spoke and performed at as well.

Around the same time we also met and were invited to interview and film with photographer Jeff Forney for a project about biological reunions called Innocent People, another fellow adoptee who was in reunion, and his doc team who had a documentary project of his own specifically about different biological reunions called *Innocent People.*

Performing with a Purpose, Caring for the Cause

All the while Don and I began receiving invites to perform for a Foster Care Awareness Mitzvah Day at Temple Aliyah, A Homeless Awareness Day at School, A private Home is Where the Heart is Program, and a public one at the Studio City Public Library. We continued to lead Shabbats sometime and performed at Several Shabbats at Malibu Jewish Community Center, as well as kept visible and around and about in local LA music venues performing in coffee shops, farmers markets, open mics, bars, and established music venues like Hotel Cafe as well as were featured in Story Corps through The Annenberg Museum.We joined Hope of the Valley and The Get Together Foundation and performed for The Weekend to End Homelessness where Don got to meet Mayor Garcetti, which later lead to Don and I creating a music and arts program called Fine Arts Revolution Program for some of the youth of the families residing in Hope of the Valley's new family housing spaces. We also were guests of and performed at The World's Biggest Sleep Out event at the Rose Bowl.

All the while still volunteering to perform and speak at Hope of the Valley's lunchtimes as well as being invited to perform, we returned a third year only now to play on the main stage for their Thanksgiving Bash.

Thanksgiving Banquet Held For Those Less Fortunate In Van Nuys

Nearly a thousand people, many of them homeless, were given a special Thanksgiving feast in the Valley.

Hermela Aregawi

Thanksgiving Banquet Held For Those Less Fortunate In Van Nuys

Nearly a thousand people, many of them homeless, were given a special Thanksgiving feast in the Valley.

This led to an interview with a local news station that spawned a second interview with ABC's news anchor Gabriella Milian which then led to an interview with Gadi Schwartz as

a national feature on NBC Nightly News and other interviews with national publications like The Epoch Times.

As we continued to volunteer and now working closely with Jeanette on programs and blogs I ultimately met fellow adoptee playwright Brian Stanton who asked me to collaborate with him with my piano compositions on his new play and film entitled *Ghost Kingdom* about the journey of the adopted self searching for birth family namely about his personal journey looking for his birth father.

Shortly after that, inspired by the multi faceted world adoptees live in, I headed back into the studio to record a song I co-wrote with songwriter producer Shane Alexander called the *Constellations* about the *Adoption Constellation*.

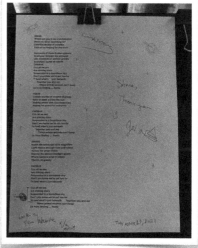

And The Years Kept Going

As the years passed on, we were able to establish a reliable routine together, each morning making a quick breakfast for Don and coffee for me, a snack with a second cigar mid day, and dinner each night. I came to discover he likes a little bit of everything and insists on sharing with the dogs yet if he were left to make meals himself, the kitchen might come undone so four years later we made a system that worked well for the both of us. About thirty minutes before I might wake, he wakes from his own space, grabs the first swisher sweet cigar I lay out for him the night before as he makes his coffee before his breakfast and eventually when I rise we convene and start the day.

During the days, I would find he likes to sit in a space behind my yard in what sort of resembles a fresher version of his old alley ways, keeping a little piece of himself always, setting up his chair in the shade, with sometimes a chess set with books, sits to smoke and chats with his spirit friends while playing dice to practicing winning. It would feel charming to me and I love the sense of just simply knowing he was there. And our adventures of family fun field trips, getting closer to one another, making music together, and sharing our reunion story with others continued on.

Adventures and Shadowing

When I think of my birth father a word that constantly comes to mind is resilience ... not just in his every way, but also simply in his every day. During the pandemic of 2020, we lost our little travel trailer and everything inside it during an unfortunate event we were lucky to of survived during the pandemic, he kept his spirit centered and was quick to accept the loss as things coming and going for him has always been just a part of life; change the constant, just another day.... what an inspiration, simply making everything better. Yet, as we healed through that experience and began putting ourselves back together we got help to upgrade to a new one and went on an amazing trip to get it and did private house concerts to support the documentary along the way.

Limo Style

We also had a rocking 60th bday for Don during the pandemic.

149

Health and Wellness

Nothing lasts forever so we make the best of every day and manage to keep health a priority. Like peas in a pod, if things get tough, we take action as a team. Regular check ups and health maintenance is always a priority. It's funny though, even as I still look after him now, our story seems to have shifted to where Don is often patiently waiting for me to find stability and security in my life as a female alone on this planet so he can finally be released from it, almost as if he is really here in my life to spiritually help and protect me. That in some ways maybe he didn't really need anything at all, and perhaps it was me who did.

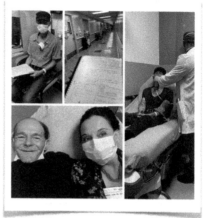

The Casino

And, I'm also not a gambler or a hustler but I have been known to mirror and manage a few... so for a "Inventor-Father's Day" hang with The Don per his request, we did exactly what he used to do and wanted to do for his special day and went to The Hustler, the Hustler and the Boss. The Boss holds the bank of investment for the initial start, converting it to a recouped reserve while managing the cash out win guiding the winnings only towards the next game played; every time (me, the shadow) and the Hustler walks in, sits down, knows when to hold em and knows when to fold em, *(Don)... needless to say, he won.

Taking It On the Road

We also partnered up with Hope of The Valley as they expanded around Los Angeles with an innovative way to transition homeless demographics into homes with new housing campuses called Tiny Homes. We toured those and then decided to take our program *Home is Where the Heart is, An Adoption and Biological Reunion Program with Story and Song* on the road around the country to share our story and song with others.

Home is Where the Heart Is
An Adoption & Biological Reunion Story with Song Tour

featuring singer songwriter Jenni Alpert
aka birth name "Cami" and her birth father Don
The Biological Duo

DENVER RESCUE MISSION

7.19.21 Los Angeles, CA ~ Hotel Cafe
7.30.21 N. Hollywood, CA ~ Hope of the Valley Rescue Mission, Chandler Tiny Homes
8.6.21 Denver, CO ~ Denver Rescue Mission, The Crossing
8.9.21 Kansas City MO ~ Rescue Mission
8.10.21 Chicago IL ~ The Olive Branch Rescue Mission
8.12.21 Detroit MI ~ Lighthouse (Rescue Missions)
8.15.21 Boston, MA ~ In Honor of Hugh McGowan
8.17.21 New York, NY ~ The Covenant House (Virtual)
8.17.21 New York, NY ~ The Bitter End
8.18.21 New York, NY ~ Rockwood Music Hall (Stage 3)
8.19.21 Philadelphia, PA~ Grape Street Pub for The Covenant House (Virtual)
8.21.21 Baltimore, MD ~ House Concert
8.22.21 The Covenant House National Sleepout for Homelessness Awareness (Virtual)
8.25.21 Atlanta, GA ~ Art Gallery w/ Cleve Willis
8.26.21 Atlanta, GA ~ Gateway Rescue Mission
8.27.21 Nashville, TN ~ Nashville Rescue Mission
8.28.21 Nashville, TN ~ Belcourt Taps
8.28.21 Nashville, TN ~ Cabana Taps w/ Aubryn
8.31.21 Basement East (New Faces)
9.2.21 Oklahoma City, OK ~ w The Imaginaries

In a world where homelessness is more prevalent today than ever, one biological reunion tackles the improbable. Years after being taken away from her birth parents by the state placed in the foster care system, then adopted at all age four, singer songwriter Jenni Alpert went searching for her birth father. She finally finds him homeless, addicted, and running from the law yet a musician just like her. "Home is Where the Heart Is a program with singer - songwriter Jenni Alpert otherwise known as her birth name Cami and her birth father Don. The Biological Duo sharing story and song which focuses on themes of homelessness, addiction, incarceration, foster care, adoption, reunification, transformation, and music through the journey of their reunion.

Homelessness . Addiction . Incarceration . Foster Care . Adoption . Biological Reunion . Transformation
www.jennialpert.com

HOPE OF THE VALLEY RESCUE MISSION   gateway Center   Covenant House   NASHVILLE RESCUE MISSION   Lighthouse

www.jennialpert.com

Home is Where the Heart Is
An Adoption & Biological Reunion Story with Song Program

featuring singer songwriter Jenni Alpert aka her birth name
"Cami" and her birth father Don - The Biological Duo

Hope of the Valley Shelters

Fri July 9th - Raymer Shelter
Fri July 16th - Pacoima Shelter
Friday July 23rd - Alexandria Campus
Fri July 30th - Chandler Campus

with Cami and Don
The Biological Duo

Lunchtime Concert
Noon

Save the Date
Hotel Cafe
Mon July 19th
7:30p

HOPE OF THE VALLEY RESCUE MISSION

Homelessness . Addiction . Incarceration . Foster Care . Adoption . Biological Reunion . Transformation
www.jennialpert.com

jenni alpert
& don logsdon

Biological Reunion

you may be my father
?

music by
jenni alpert
@ghostkingdom

CONSTELLATIONS
JENNI ALPERT

Big Picture Purpose

I knew from the start that Don's energy and his capacity to learn set him in a good position to be inspired if he was just presented with options and opportunities in a certain way. Looking at Don was, for me, a reflection of myself; he was me if I had not had the tools, the opportunities, the stability and the love I had been given. And together we hope to make a difference for others.

Don: *"Though there are some parts of me that will and can never change, since I've met my daughter I am without a doubt a new person. She has let me get extremely close to her and I love and am grateful for every minute of it."*

In the last four and a half years we have done everything from going skydiving and ice skating, to watching movies with homemade meals and drinking delicious coffee together, to going to hear some of Don's favorite bands like Robin Trower, Ozzy, and some of mine; Rob Zombie and Guns and Roses, and gone shopping at health food stores together. We've also spent quality time staring out on the horizon just gazing at the stars out under the open sky. We've played music together and spoken to groups about our story and transformation proving to be the most thrilling life journey for me ever. I have had the opportunity to get to know this man in a way I never thought I would and we have learned about profoundness and love as we experience togetherness and closeness based on a sense of understanding and trust that we built together. This formed a bond for me that will not and cannot be broken. Don has guided me, supported me through so much, and loved me for no reason other than I am who I am. It can't get much better than that.

Don: *"Since Cami came into my life she has guided me through a new sense of routine and shown me a lot, though some things took a lot longer than before. She helped me do more than you know, she got me off of probation for good, helped me to stabilize my life, and even now she makes sure I have meals, coffee, books, chess, music, and adventure with space to myself each day I feel good knowing she is there. I've never much been a people person and always chose to be alone on my own. And I would never say that my life before was wrong or bad, but my life right now is fuller because I've gotten to see so many things with my daughter and I don't have to worry about getting into trouble every day anymore. Things in my life are going on in such a way that I had never even known before. I also can say I could of never raised her the way the Alpert's did and I never could of given her this life either. I'm actually grateful for them. This way of life is sure really different but I wouldn't change anything for the time now with my her."*

I didn't ask Don to change. I didn't invite him to do anything but if I can open a door of ideas and understanding for him to decide what he wants for himself, then I want to do it and I am proud of the way this approach worked out for us. I think that the greatest gift one can give is to love people in the way that you yourself may never have been loved and love them for who they are and for the best they can be; in a way that fills up all of the unreasonable doubt and questions you may have had. In this way, we get the opportunity to show someone what is referred to as *'unconditional love.'* But this really should just be the love that belongs to everyone; it's the love that we all deserve. And the emptiness from my childhood has grown old. The adult me is so warm and filled with so much love and gratefulness. I am so fortunate to have a fantastic adoptive family as well as this new connection to my biological past. The man who now stands at the top of the mountain of transformation really doesn't need to transform at all – for it is really just a matter of remembering and choosing; for love is, in fact, the wings of freedom we give others, and for each other we do exactly that.

Don: *"As it is true one time long ago I said to myself that in the event that if you were born I wouldn't be able to be there for you and raise you, but it is also true that I said that I would meet you later in life and once I did I would give you everything I had and do everything I could for you for the rest of my days.... one message I wrote down to myself that I actually lived up to and made good on."*

I am now really feel whole and fulfilled because I know that in my life is one of the most incredible and amazing men I have ever met: my biological father. Sometimes, late at night I find myself preparing for life without Don, knowing that I may outlive all the people I love in my life one day, trying to remember what life was like before I met him. And sometimes I ask myself was he an apparition, a long dream I just had, this experience so completely profound. But what seems to settle most in my mind are all the profound person moments we share, invaluable lessons I've learned, and that nothing is quite what it seems. That it's never about what we have or where we live that defines us, that life is about cherishing the people in it, and the sense of home and belonging we may long for is found where the heart is. That in fact, in the act of transformation we may simply be reverting back to who we really are, who we are meant to be, and who we are to become when love and understanding is there to remind us.

Don: "If there was one thing I'd want to tell my daughter, it would be, "Thank you, I love "you."

155

FOSTER A FUTURE; AN ADOPTION CONSTELLATION

There are 107,918 foster children eligible for and waiting to be adopted. In 2014, 50,644 foster kids were adopted — a number that has stayed roughly consistent for the past five years. The average age of a waiting child is 7.7 years old and 29% of them will spend at least three years in foster care…

Foster Care and Adoption

1. How Many Children Are Waiting to be Adopted?

There are 107,918 foster children eligible for and waiting to be adopted. In 2014, 50,644 foster kids were adopted — a number that has stayed roughly consistent for the past five years. The average age of a waiting child is 7.7 years old and 29% of them will spend at least three years in foster care.

The AFCARS report shows that more American families are responding to the call to adopt, as 63,123 children were adopted from foster care in FY 2018—a 6% increase in the past year and the highest number of adoptions in the history of the report.

Resource

https://adoptioncouncil.org/article/your-guide-to-2018s-foster-care-statistics

2. How Many Children are Actually Adopted in the US Alone?

About 135,000 children are adopted in the United States each year. Of non-stepparent adoptions, about 59% are from the child welfare (or foster) system, 26% are from other countries, and 15% are voluntarily relinquished American babies.

Resource

https://adoptionnetwork.com/knowledge-hub/adoption-myths-facts/domestic-us-statistics

3. Foster Care Today

According to the most recent federal data, there are currently more than 400,000 children in foster care in the United States today. They range in age from infants to 21 years old (in some states). The average age of a child in foster care is more than 8 years old, and there are slightly more boys than girls.

Resource
https://www.adoptuskids.org/meet-the-children/children-in-foster-care/about-the-children

4. Age of Adoption
If we include all children under 5, we're looking at almost half of all adoptions (49%). On the other hand, teenagers (13 - 17) account for less than 10% of all adoptions. While there are fewer teenagers waiting to be adopted, as a whole, they are less likely to be adopted than younger children.

Resource
https://partnersforourchildren.org/blog/what-does-age-have-do-adoption-0

5. How often do biological reunions work out?
Many reunions take from five to eight years or more to "normalize" and reach a stage where the participants have built up shared memories and familiar relationships.

Resource
https://www.americanadoptioncongress.org/docs/etiquette8_.pdf

6. Should we have a biological reunion?
Not everyone wants an adoption reunion.
Sometimes birth parents or adult adoptees simply have no strong desire to reconnect after the adoption. Other times, they don't feel emotionally ready for such a step. Some people harbor negative feelings about the closed adoption and haven't been able to resolve those feelings.

An adoption reunion may not be the best choice for yourself or for the person you're trying to reconnect with. Adoption reunions can bring complicated, long-buried emotions back to the surface. Not everyone is willing to, ready to, or able to process these feelings. So an adoption reunion should be very carefully considered before you take any action to reunite.

7. How to Approach an Adoption Reunion with Biological Family Members

This is where things can get even trickier. If you've successful managed to find your birth mother or an adult adoptee through your adoption search (which can sometimes be difficult, depending on how much information you start with), initiating contact with them might be even more difficult.

It's scary to contact someone who you're biologically related to, but who is essentially a stranger to you. Several things can happen. You'll need to be prepared for any of these possibilities before you decide whether or not to request a reunion after adoption. Have someone you trust to support you! Talk to other adoptees or birth family members who've reunited after adoption to hear their adoption reunion stories.

Resource
https://www.americanadoptions.com/blog/adoption-reunions-what-to-expect

8. What is The Adoption Constellation
Author: Michael Phillip Grand, PhD

The Adoption Constellation is the systemic concept of the constellation is used to demonstrate that interpersonal relationships beyond the nuclear adoptive family influence the primary relationships between adoptive and birth parents and their children written by Michael Grand. The Adoption Constellation provides an in-depth analysis of the foundational principles of our cultural and psychological understanding of adoption. The systemic concept of the constellation is used to demonstrate that interpersonal relationships beyond the nuclear adoptive family influence the primary relationships between adoptive and birth parents and their children. Questioning the adequacy of the theory of Primal Wound to explain adoptive experience, a more culturally-grounded understanding of adoption is offered. Grand surveys the literature on adoption and stigma, demonstrating that the experience of adoption cannot be divorced from a community's assessment of the status of this family form. Integrating the cultural and psychological factors influencing the experience of adoption, the social construction of narrative identity is used to capture the lived experience of members of the adoption constellation. Core themes such as loss, rejection, grief, intimacy, and mattering are described. The book concludes with an analysis of alternatives beyond conventional adoption as a basis for permanency, and a suggested set of political strategies for opening up adoption records.

Resource
http://www.kinshipcenter.org/education-institute/education-store/the-adoption-constellation-new-ways-of-thinking-about-and-practicing-adoption.html

9. What are the Seven Core Issues in Adoption and Permanency?

Authors: Sharon Roszia and Alison Davis-Maxon

The Seven Core Issues are Loss, Rejection, Shame/Guilt, Grief, Identity, Intimacy, and Mastery/Control. The book expands the model to be inclusive of adoption and all forms of permanency: adoption, foster care, kinship care, donor insemination, and surrogacy. Attachment and trauma are integrated with the Seven Core Issues model to address and normalize the additional tasks individuals and families will encounter.

Resources from the book - The Seven Core Issues in Adoption and Permanency? A Comprehensive Guide to Promoting Understanding and Healing In Adoption, Foster Care, Kinship Families, and Third-Party Reproduction

10. What is is the Adoption Revolution and how is it Transforming Our Families and America?

Author, Adam Pertman

"What I learned as a result of adopting – and even more from writing my first book, Adoption Nation was that the legal, social and moral playing field in the realm of child welfare (including adoption) is not level or fair to any of the parties involved, especially not adoptees or their birth/first parents." The history and human impact of adoption and the corrosive myths surrounding it and the issues adoptees grapple relating to race, identity, equality, discrimination, personal history, and connections with all their families are all valuable elements to focus on with regard to adoption writes author Adam Pertman with compassion for adopted individuals and adoptive and birth parents alike, an adoptive parent of two himself. For the first edition of this groundbreaking examination of adoption and its impact on us all, Pertman won awards from many organizations, including the American Academy of Child and Adolescent Psychiatrists, the Dave Thomas Center for Adoption Law, the American Adoption Congress, the Century Foundation, Holt International, and the U.S. Congress. In this updated edition, Pertman reveals how changing attitudes and laws are transforming adoption - and thereby American society - in the twenty-first century.

Resource

11. Understanding the Transition from Foster Care to Adoption

From a Personal and Professional Perspective by Jeanette Yoffe, M.A., M.F.T.

The transition from foster care to adoption can be very difficult for a child and there are many challenges to take into consideration. The challenges center around separation and loss, trust, rejection, guilt and shame, identity, intimacy, loyalty, and mastery or power and control. I will primarily be dealing with children between the ages of six and twelve and their developmental stages. Followed by ways in which parents and therapists can understand how to help a foster or adopted child cope with these psychological complexities so the transition can be smoother for all involved.

Resource

https://celiacenter.org/understanding-adoption-foster-care/

12. How Can We Support All Those in The Foster Care and Adoption Constellation?

Celia Center is a California non-profit center that nurtures and supports all members of the foster-adoption constellation by providing emotional, educational, and community engagement via support groups, conferences, arts festivals, wolf healings, and trainings. The monthly open support group is called Adopt Salon which is designed for all members of the Adoption Constellation: First-Birth Parents, Adoptees, Former Foster Youth, Foster Parents, Legal Guardians, Adoptive Parents and Kinship Families. This monthly support group is a place for the Adoption & Foster Care community to come together to share stories, thoughts, feelings, ideas, receive psycho-education, process grief/loss, learn about search and reunion, and build strong bonds/connections facilitated by Founder, Fellow Formerly Fostered and Adopted, Adoption Psychotherapist, Adult Adoptee Jeanette Yoffe, MFT.

Resources and more on Celia Center

https://celiacenter.org/history-of-celia-center-milestones/

Quotes

Foster Care, Adoption, Reunions, The Adopted Self
Jeanette Yoffe

"Adoptees have an onion shell persona, the primal wound is one layer, but it's not the whole onion. There is so much more! The onion shell metaphor is the lifelong discovery of being open to growth, developing new layers of experience and new ways to identify the self as not one, but many."

"A belief system becomes internalized unless deemed otherwise."

"With the highs of "reunion" also comes the deep feelings of loss at the life you didn't have with the people you were born from."

"It is important to tell the child that "sometimes we will not know all the answers but we at least have a place to hold the questions other than inside us all the time to help carry the load."

"When you become angry and intense, it means you care deeply."

"We don't get over grief, we get used to it."

Sometimes we're so caught up in our own "traumas' that we are incapable of receptive listening.

It's not what's wrong with us, it's about what happened to us."

"We need balance within our self, in order to balance the self in others."

"Our brains are wired for WE."

LETTERS AND SALUTATIONS

Aug 14, 2017 : Hello, my name is Jenni Alpert (legal) / Jennifer Alpert and also Cameron (Cami) Morantz (intended biological name), I am Don Logsdon's daughter, and I wanted to introduce myself and share a bit about our story....

Letters for Don

Aug 14, 2017

Hello, my name is Jenni Alpert (legal) / Jennifer Alpert and also Cameron (Cami) Morantz (intended biological name), I am Don Logsdon's daughter, and I wanted to introduce myself and share a bit about our story. I was born in September to a Mary Lou Morantz and a Don Logsdon and quickly was placed in the foster care system days after having been born due to both of them being wards of the state as a mean of protection and redirection for the fate of my life and finally adopted by the Alpert's at about age 4.

About a year and a half ago, after having learned about both Mary Lou and Don's individual histories and past, as well as of Mary Lou's life and death, having spent about seven years acquainting myself with her family members as the first form of a biological reunion and reconnection of sorts, I decided to look up the possible whereabouts of the remaining biological parent I had, my biological father Don Logsdon. After extensive preliminary research before meeting Don, and years of social service volunteering to obtain field work training independently in areas of homelessness and management of 'mental wellness' and social skills issues, rehabilitating incarcerated inmates building by developing a rehabilitation program that utilized music and the arts for the downtown men's correctional facility, aiding youth trapped in prostitution seeking protection, having worked closely with foster children helping them to develop independence and life skills during and after emancipation, working privately as a special needs tutor shadow for children with unique abilities and autism, and having done intensive study on drug addiction, use, abuse and the chronic criminal activity connected, I felt prepared and patience enough to choose to see if Don was still alive and in a place to meet me, his biological daughter if for no other reason but to learn of each others lives here on earth and to say hello.

Last year on July 26, 2016 I found Don, who at the time was running from the law and still committing crimes as usual while living partly in a dog run alley of sorts on the side of a long beach dwelling and part time by freeway underpasses in bushes near a casino in between California prisons and jails with a warrant out for his arrest for another violation of his probation. And he was using a plethora of street drugs and prescription medication to boot. While I scouted out the Long Beach dwelling in advance before meeting Don face to face, I was offered an opportunity to read through some of Don's early letters to his family written from prison, and in between the lines of his words I could sense a person who never had an opportunity to see another perspective of live than the ones he had been shown at an early age embedded with poverty, lack of supervision and parenting guidance, and living spaces hoarded with trash, rats, cockroaches, and drugs, yet somehow there was a hint of hope for kindness and love. I chose to show up every day for three weeks last summer ranging from 3-8 hours a day spending time observing Don in his current state allowing and accepting him to be exactly who he was and where he was in his life with open arms. My instincts told me that early on the Long Beach police patrol were aware of my presence. During those first three weeks of what I refer to as on site field work, I began to take Don on many family fun field trips, first short and small dates to build trust and rapport. It didn't take long for us to bond over music, chess, craft coffee, reading, and exploring libraries, beaches, parks, and many recreational activities to establish a bond of similarities while exposing Don too many new experiences. It was at this point Don chose to turn himself in on his own and also decided to decline his use and eventually stop taking street drugs and prescribed narcotics altogether without my request or guidance in those departments.

Our story continues on for an entire year now with what I believe to be more future to unfold with many details to share to date, some already documented online through series of photos, videos, and written accounts, with more future documentation to come, and I am both forever grateful for these opportunities and experiences and excited to continue to share more in hopes that perhaps others may be helped one day as well. Yet at this time, I want to take a moment to focus on, recognize, and express my deepest gratitude, appreciation, and thanks to Don's final probation officer Officer B and her supervisor, both the Long Beach and Los Angeles Police departments and the individual men in the force who assisted by truly supporting me on various steps of this incredible and creative journey, and for the Judge and Courts for taking time out not only to deal with Don's repetitive case, but also for having granted Don the chance and allowance to be with me this year and to creatively try something different in life and perhaps unheard possibilities and approaches for a possible rewiring and rehabilitation.

It is because of all of you that this was allowed to unfold as it did and I not only salute you for your team work and openness but also for your excellence.

Thank you, Cami - Don Logsdon's biological daughter
AKA Jenni Alpert

On Fri, Nov 11, 2016 at 5:37 AM
Jenni Alpert wrote: Subject: Important things to know about Don re living at the sober house / his recovery which is actually discovery and wellness spectrum details / our choices / why I am a shadow and guardian for him

Hi all, this is a heads up with very important notes about Don (this will appear long but is important): We are choosing to try out this transitional space at this time because the environment and recovery perimeters appear to be a positive fit for Don's development and recovery style. His situation is not mainly about drug abuse as it is about obtaining life development and experience in a safe non oppressive yet wellness aware place. I will be his shadow and guardian during this new self reliance phase and self discovery phase and we will be working on many things including social skills and aspects of mental wellness spectrum awareness and skills, please use me as a resource at every turn and please understand the magnitude and value of my recommendations and requests for safety and stability.

1. Don has a cough partly from cigar smoke that I am aware of which surfaces especially at night and when he sleeps on his back. He does knows to roll on his side to keep from choking right away and to not swallow but may not always remember instantly at the noise of the cough. It's ok. He will eventually remember. Please don't let the coughing disturb you or make health suggestions. He can not take certain medicine yet (even if he asks for it which he probably won't) while on probation and his health is being monitored. Please call me right away if there is any need for help of any kind.

2. Please don't encourage anyone in the house to make suggestions to Don - especially to take him places. Only G has approval to drive him anywhere other than myself for legal and safety reasons. Close by walks are fine but most of the time he will go alone. Although he is public transit savvy I would prefer he not use this yet. We are working off old habits and keeping him safe and far away from old dangerous areas and spaces that could trigger him. Please notify me first about suggestions or desired outings if they are of interest for safety reasons. Please don't pay for him to do activities without notifying me first. We are in the early stages of building a relationship to money the value of such earning and spending in healthy ways, as well as the value of nice purchases and regulating use of simple things like shared toilet paper as simple as this seems to anyone else and any positive experience would benefit him greatly for these things to be part of this process.

3. Please help others be kind and understanding. His social development is not always obvious due to his charm, chosen shyness, and talents and I am in the process of helping him learn and develop these among other things regarding self care and mental wellness upkeep (social skills, verbal choices and general meanings facial expressions tone of voice eye contact and reactions). His memory in certain areas is also not strong.

It is my hope that others in the house don't make many suggestions, advise, or give him ideas about anything - especially regarding activities or travel outside the house, jobs since he will need specific types and experience (he has never once had an actual job and tho he can teach chess and play music extremely well he has never had any formal training of any kind), money (it's not time for banking yet, medical or SSI talk, general purchases especially cell phones. We will be transitioning into this - computers electronics and so on (he has never had money, is still developing this and management of this and most of his things have always gotten stolen so we

164

will be working on this together outside of the house, or anything car and driving related. Please refrain from anything other than sharing about one's own self if asked and please pass along the message to others in the house to do the same for safety reasons. It won't be productive.

4. I am also aware of his memory relapse as he won't some remember things day to day. Please if you notice anything not regularly done, remind him "kindly" about dishes and cleanliness, general time (he doesn't nor has ever had a watch or used alarms, prison did this for him so for the most part I'll help him kindly),

5. Finally, you may notice from time to time vocal volume when overly upset that he may not be heard or understood, excited or overwhelmed - (please do not let any man take this personally - he doesn't always notice and can not help this yet). For important things like the Sun Night meeting kindly remind or mention them. I will be doing the same for him daily and will make sure to get him up for important time things like work.

Thanks so much,
Cami - biological name (Use)
Jenni - legal name (for record)

On Oct 17, 2016, at 5:08 PM,
@shakespearecenter> wrote:

Thank you so much for sharing the joy, and heartbreak, but mostly joy in these photos. How amazing that you & your father both seem to connect strongly with music! I hope that your relationship continues to grow in love and transformation.

Best, Chris

Subject: Hi! Info
Hey there Chris,

Wanted to say a very big thank you for everything you did for me and letting me receive some letters there. All is well and Don is doing great. I was able to get him into a sober living home in the valley so I moved that way in order to be closer to him. I may get another letter to your way from the jail due to milk delay so if I do please let me know and I will happily come and pick it up.

Otherwise many thanks.
Cami / Jenni

█████

From: jenni alpert
Date: October 20, 2016 at 4:23:23 PM PDT
To: @earthlink
Subject: Thank you for the meeting

Thank you so much for meeting with Don today.

If you have the time to write us an email that states that you met with Don in a sort of interview process of recovery home options that I can use as part of his profile for his Probation officer and personal use that would really be great.

As for Cornerstone, we will happily check it out Monday after hearing back from J.

Thank You!
Cami / Jenni

Date: October 31, 2016 at 2:52:22 PM PDT
To: Laurie Craft
Subject: Re: Today's large feat - the Probation Officer impromptu meeting.

Hi Laurie,

Thanks SO much. In fact you can help.

I would super appreciate any and all help obtaining a list of sober living with optional mental wellness resources of no force of any sort that are free or extremely of low income or work to live option if you know of any that we can visit and view. We are also open to AB109 supported venues if they are a match for Don's personality and case file. By observation, Don can successfully share a room with one other male however, would but would do best alone. He will need the freedom to have visits from me as well as optional off site family wellness field trips all the while having some sense of structure with the basic amenities: shower, hot meals, work opportunities, possible classes,

FYI, He has a legit medical marijuana permit instead of having to take psych meds that he is willing to try for now, and is able to work efficiently for about 5-6 hours about 3 days a week in exchange for cash or other services with his janitorial, basic cooking and clean up, and basic gardening skills. Thanks so much for your help and recommendations.

Cami / Jenni Alpert
Sent from my iPhone

On Oct 31, 2016, at 2:38 PM,
Laurie Craft wrote:

Hi Jenni (Cami),
I am SO HAPPY to hear that! I am confident that Don's continued journey of recovery and emotional wellness is all going to fall into place, especially with you advocating for him. Let me know if we can help with anything!

Laurie Craft | Site Director-Help Center | Hope of the Valley

Date: October 21, 2016 at 1:14:05 AM PDT To: Officer RL

Subject: Hope of the Valley recovery option Hi Officer L,

One follow up for today to send your way before I call his actual probation officer tomorrow for the email and information on what is acceptable in terms of amount of contact and follow up since I know you are all busy in this world, but also to ask some of the questions Don had to see what route are best to continue on this journey. Enclosed below are some photos of Don with me helping foster children write music. He did a great job. Have a good night and many thanks for your time.

Cami / Jenni

▬▬

From: jenni alpert
Date: October 10, 2016 at 2:13:52 PM PDT To: @beittshuvah
Subject: Confirming appointment for Don Logsdon
Fri Oct 14th - 9am Hi J,

Don received your message today and tried to call back but didn't want to leave a message in the general mailbox for concern it may get lost and looked but couldn't find your extension #. I hope sending you an email is ok.

*From Don ---> Hi J.
Thank you for your message.
I will be there on this Friday 10-14 at 9a.
Don

▬▬

From: jenni alpert
Date: August 1, 2016 at 10:51:56 PM PDT To: @beittshuvah
Subject: Hi - thanks so much for speaking w me Friday and Hello,

I wanted to update you on the status of my biological father. Today we went to the Los Angeles public library, read children's books together, he filled out his very first library card application, played some guitar and listened as well, visited the WW2 museum at the library, learned how banks work, saw some live music together and ate BBQ - he covered his every bill and I did not accept any gift during our whole day. Also exclaimed that he couldn't believe how much time passed and he didn't use.

He called and spoke to R and left a message for M regarding intake should he qualify. He has done some very hard criminal time and is addicted to hard drugs with absolutely no history of a day and exposure to a life like this ever before in his life. He is highly intelligent and open yet in a very very dangerous situation where he lives and how he operates with other local drug addicts and is walking the thinnest fine criminal line that even an situational mistake could be detrimental to any rehabilitation -

To me this isn't even about second chance - it's about giving someone a real first chance if in fact the karma is his to do. From the time I have spent with him thus far despite how hard it will be, I know he will be worth the investment in. We hope to meet to visit you very very soon.

Don's Daughter
Cami / Jenni Alpert

███

On May 24, 2017, at 6:25 AM
Jenni Alpert wrote:

Good Morning Officer B,

I am inquiring about the SSI interview and a follow up from the previous call as we have not yet heard back yet from assistance regarding the proper steps to take in order to get the ball rolling for Don's SSI application. I am new to this and want to make sure I don't make any mistakes in guiding Don through this stage. When you or 360 have time, any help to get the ball rolling for him would be great. I really appreciate this.

Best,
Cami / Jenni

███

5-9-2017

Hi Officer B,

We received a call from J at 360 this morning and began the research process for the next few steps in Don's progress, thank you so much. I was wondering if it was possible to obtain a copy of the court transcripts from 4-10 from you on Thurs for our files as the public defender showed us the information and we returned it to him this time.

Otherwise all is status quo, Many thanks
Cami/ Jenni Alpert

███

3-20-2017
Received From Officer B

Are you still attending the Hope of the Valley Rescue Mission and if so how often and what are you participating in? Is there anything you would like addressed in the report? Are you still going to the Cornerstone program? If so how often and what are you participating in?

Thank you

2-27-2017
Received from Officer B

> That's less than 48 hours so you can go, just email me when you leave and when you get back.

███

From: Jenni Alpert
Sent: Wednesday, February 22, 2017 3:39 PM To: Officer B
Subject: Re: All good, quick q thx

> 7- 8 hours prob with driving give or take.
Sent from my iPhone

On Feb 22, 2017, at 3:09 PM,
Officer B wrote:

> How long do you plan to be there?

███

From: Jenni Alpert
Sent: Wednesday, February 22, 2017 1:49 PM To: Officer B
Subject: All good, quick q thx Hi Officer B

> All is well here, thanks again for your extra time the last we came in. In our need to use the bathroom, I forgot to request a day form to take Don to Big Bear sometime soon to see the snow. In looking at the calendar and the weather, next Thurs Mar 2 might be a nice day to go. What would the most efficient process be to fill out a travel permit? Also wanted to confirm that during our next appointment on Mar 9th that we can set up the meeting for filling out the SSI paperwork and any other GR forms that may apply to Don for his future with the office you mentioned.

Many thanks
Cami / Jenni

███

1-13-2017
Received from Officer B

> Wednesday would be fine, at 2pm. See you then.

███

From: Jenni Alpert
Sent: Friday, January 13, 2017 10:34 AM To: Officer B
Subject: Hi! mlk weekend Hi Officer B,

> Hope all is well with you this fine Friday. As I had suspected when I double checked the calendar today I realized this special weekend is an honor of MLK which means that our initial meeting to stop by and see you on Monday for the permission slip will need to be pushed till Wednesday due to the holiday should that be OK with you and

should that make sense with the holiday for your office.

If Wednesday at any point works best for you next week to pick up the permission slip for SF, I was also wondering if you would be willing to spend a few extra minutes with us helping us through the process of learning how to apply properly for SS I and SSDI - perhaps someone in your office or in your network may have experience in applying for both of these things as when we met with a offsite caseworker to interview her skill set to help us through the process it turned out she really didn't have experience enough at all. It is my feeling at this time that applying for SSI and SSD to learn how to use a bank for the first time with me as the conservator is a great next step before researching and applying for any type of section 8 low income housing should that even be something Don would be interested later on down the line. Nonetheless putting him on a list upon researching environments that may match his preference could be a good idea to research as well at some point. Between you and I from my four month daily observation I believe that some of Don struggles are related to experiences from having been institutionalized in and out of the system from the age of eight until 54 years old in addition to childhood abuse and neglect. His transformation and growth in this short period of time is mesmerizing and a positive reflection of his ability to manage his future freedom yet while we have this next three month window I believe it would be beneficial to prepare him for society as much as possible despite his personal preference of how he chooses to interact with them later. Therefore any additional government services and benefits we should be aware of that you may suggest would also be welcome. Your help would be greatly appreciated if you have the time.

In the meantime for this particular holiday weekend I was thinking it might be fun to take Don somewhere out of LA for a day or two to learn more about Martin Luther King at the African museum downtown Los Angeles first and then to see different historical spots neighboring Los Angeles perhaps slightly south to the town of Julian or if we chose to go north instead perhaps Solvang camping the evening of this Saturday night. I believe either destination are slightly out of the 50 mile radius so I was wondering if there was a way to do this for the holiday weekend and if not it's no problem there are plenty of other places we can stay much closer until our SF trip. If you have time open this coming Wednesday instead of holiday Monday let me know what time works for you either the 11 o'clock hour, noon, 1, or 2 will work for us.

Best wishes and hear from you soon thank you
Cami / Jenni

■

I have forwarded your email to DPO B. She could direct you in the right direction. She will be in the office tomorrow.
Very happy for your father. He is very fortunate to have you.

RL
Deputy Probation Officer
Los Angeles County Probation Department

Hi Cami/Jenni,

I spoke with J C, one of our case managers today, and she is available to meet with Don next Thursday, January 12 at 10:00am. She may not have too many answers in regard to SSI, our Healthcare Advocates Rep. handles all of that, but she certainly can answer questions and help guide you both. Let me know if that works on your end!

Laurie Craft | Site Director-Help Center
Hope of The Valley

██

On Jan 4, 2017, at 3:30 PM
Jenni Alpert wrote:

Would next Thurs Jan 12th after Don's court date (which by now should keep him in the same program for probation until Aug 2017) be a good time to set up an appointment with a social worker to educate ourselves properly and inquire about obtaining SSI as well as other general relief options. It may be a few more months before Don is actually ready for anything related to low income housing or bank management so please let whoever know in advance that he has never lived alone with responsibilities, never has had a bank account, and is still developing a consistent nature to following social protocol, managing time, and impulse control when making long term decisions.

This first meeting will focus mainly on setting Don up with social services (he already has food stamps and a sort of General Relief from a past application that will soon halt and a new more clear and directly relatable to Don's new reality case should be opened most likely with only SSI in a way that Don will relate to and feel safe with. We may inquire about information regarding low income housing options for educational purposes but I am pretty sure it is still too soon at this time to move to that level. Until then, it is our hope that Don will continue to split his time with me registered as homeless while continuing to test the waters at the Burbank Bridge Transitional Home with me as his social skills shadow as long as G will have his presence there when he feels safe and consistent to stay there as Don agrees to continue to do do his volunteer to live exchange on Fridays for this next window of transition.

With that said, please let us know if Thurs. of next week works for you and what time as well as if and when we may be able to offer a lunch time music concert for you.

Many thanks,
Cami / Jenni

██

Sent from my iPhone
On Jan 3, 2017, at 2:49 PM,
Laurie Craft wrote:

Hi Cami,

I am so happy to hear that Don is doing well, and that he has life goals that he wishes to attain in the new year. I always love to see people grow and blossom, and Don is certainly doing that. I think it would be a good idea to have Don meet with one of our case managers to see what other programs might be a good fit for him. They refer out to different programs depending on current benefits, need, etc. We do have a representative from Healthcare Advocates who is here at the Help Center every Tuesday at 12:00pm who can help with Social Security as well. How soon would you like to set up the appointment? I will check with our case managers to see when they are available. One is out sick today but she should be back tomorrow.

Happy New Year Cami!

Wishing you all the best in 2017!
Laurie Craft | Site Director-Help Center

On Jan 2, 2017, at 10:07 AM
Jenni Alpert wrote:

Hi Laurie!

Happy New Year, hope your trip went well and that all is

positive for Hope of The Valley in this fresh new year. As you may know Don Logsdon has expressed a huge amount of appreciation and thanks your way for all of your support and resources since we happened upon your office that fateful day of visiting the onsite AA meeting not so randomly after all perhaps.

Upon writing some new year's resolutions, Don and I have been talking some and after lots of field work towards assimilation and observation re progress, I was wondering if you and your staff social worker would be open to having a meeting with us exploring and regarding researching social service options as well as the possibility of applying for SSI after learning the pros and cons for Don's specific case. We are entering a new phase this year towards independence and self reliance upon the new introductory first time life discoveries Don obtained over the last four months to increase his choices and problem solving tools with new options to override old unsafe familiar behavioral patterns of survival and verbal descriptions of needs, feelings, wants, and boundaries thereof. After the court date of Jan 10th, it appears that Don has some great life goals he wishes to focus on and one of them includes testing out the transitional living sober men's home on a more regular basis utilizing public transportation here and there with positive motivations in conjunction with continuing to register as temporarily homeless as his safety net while he continues to develop a sense of safety and the tools to express them socially. We are grateful for your continued support in these department, thank you so very much for the trial period for a unique approach at social skill building thus far.

From shadowing and observing him every Friday for the last two and a half months during his volunteer work exchange at the Granada Hills Church donation drop off location for his trial time at the transitional men's sober living home, I have been able to evaluate his growth in focus and basic job skill level in security and location management. With a work manager on duty and flexible focus breaks during downtime while on the job, Don is very capable of switching into professional focus to represent the job and to fulfill the duties. He is polite and effective when greeting the item drop off clients and follows basic protocol. At some points location restriction guidelines and reasoning may need reminding but upon rational reminding Don is very compliant.

In addition with regards to independence building and exercising self reliance skills in new situations upon learning such new tools and the value of them in his adult life, with the possible help of an on site social worker, we will soon be ready to begin the research and development process of evaluating what exactly Don is legally and legitimately qualified to apply for, as well as learning the pros and cons to acquiring SSI, other government resources, part time jobs in fields of teaching chess, playing music for churches and nonprofits, and basic security location management positions with management on site with him opportunities, future low income housing options with possible onsite or nearby assistance and resources that may or may not fit Don's needs, capabilities, and comforts in efforts to try and match some of his own personal ideas within the scope and pace with which he can handle and commit to consistently.

Finally we are excited to perform for Hope of The Valley sometime soon this year and look forward to setting up a meeting with you and your staff soon. Please let me know should you need anything. Rehabilitation is going effectively, thank you again so very much.

Many thanks and gratitude,

Sincerely,
Don's Daughter
Cami / Jenni Alpert

███

From: Jenni Alpert
Sent: Tuesday, December 27, 2016 3:52 PM
Subject: Question for you re Don Logsdon / a documentary

Hi Officer L
I wanted to introduce you to Irene, a documentarian who took an interest in my reunited relationship with Don my biological father. Being that you are familiar with your staff and protocol, I thought to introduce you first re her inquiry to possibly attend Don's court date on Jan 10th. I have yet to obtain the information pertaining to this until the next meeting however, Irene may have questions regarding permission and protocol that I wanted to put out there should you have time and know of one.

Many thanks
Cami (AKA Jenni Alpert)

███

12-14-2016

Hi Officer L,
Hope all is well with you.
Don and I scheduled and drop in to see Officer B today briefly to obtain a family field trip permission slip to Big Bear (or possibly Santa Barbara) for Don's Bday tomorrow as well as I am starting to deliver her the paper trial process for Don's court date on Jan 10th. I wanted to shoot her an email to let her know we will come sometime before 2:30pm.

Thanks so much,
Cami / Jenni

███

Hi Cami,

My pleasure! He is a sweetheart, and I was told plays a mean guitar! I will let the
planning committee know that he offered to play on Thanksgiving. Also, if he ever
wants to play during lunch at the Help Center we would love that too!

Laurie Craft | Site Director-Help Center

███

From: Jenni Alpert
Date: January 10, 2017 at 8:42:50 AM PST
To: r.l@probation.lacounty.gov, Officer B
Subject: Arrived.

███

From: Jenni Alpert
Date: December 24, 2016 at 10:56:46 AM PST To: r.l@probation.lacounty.gov, Officer B
Subject: Update and Holiday Greeting

Thank you deeply for granting us this opportunity to develop a relationship and
explore new territory together. You and your staff have helped piece a family back
together. Healthy holidays to you and yours,

Thank you,
Cami / Jenni

███

From: Jenni Alpert
Date: December 14, 2016 at 10:18:39 AM PST To: R L
Subject: Hi! Pls Forward to Officer B for our stop in later
today

Hi Officer L,
Hope all is well with you. Don and I scheduled and drop in to see Officer B today briefly
to obtain a family field trip permission slip to Big Bear (or possibly Santa Barbara) for
Don's Bday tomorrow as well as I am starting to deliver her the paper trial process for
Don's court date on Jan 10th. I wanted to shoot her an email to let her know we will
come sometime before 2:30pm.

Thanks so much,
Cami / Jenni

From: Jenni Alpert
Date: December 8, 2016 at 2:04:29 PM PST To: R L
Subject: Re: Don Logsdon - For anyone interested who may of missed this share: Home Is
Where My Heart Is: An Adoption Story- Part I-III

Oh thank you Officer L. It is with the help of your staff and team that allowed this to
continue to happen.

Cami / Jenni

On Dec 8, 2016, at 1:46 PM, R L wrote:
Amazing and inspiring story. I am so happy for both of you.
R L
Deputy Probation Officer
Los Angeles County Probation Department

From: Jenni Alpert
Sent: Thursday, December 08, 2016 1:02 PM To: R L
Subject: Re: Don Logsdon - For anyone interested who may of missed this share: Home Is
Where My Heart Is: An Adoption Story- Part I-III
For Officer L, Officer B, and Don's judge: Don's first Job.
Grok Nation Article

From: Jenni Alpert
Date: December 8, 2016 at 11:22:15 AM PST To: r.l@probation.lacounty.gov
Subject: Photos For Officer B re her request for the Judge
RE Jan 10, 2017 8:30a court date Dec 8, 2016

Please forward to Officer B, thank you. Officer B & Officer R,
Here is a selection of photos to forward to the judge along with the papers I will be
dropping off next Wed to help prepare for Don's court date in advance. Couldn't decide
what to pick so here is a selection for you. Hope you both have a wonderful week,

Thank you
Cami

From: Jenni Alpert
Date: November 30, 2016 at 11:13:15 AM PST
To: R L
Subject: Re: question and update Hi Officer L,

We completed the Dr. Visit. Enclosed is the paperwork for the visit, diagnosis, and
antibiotic / inhaler for bronchial infection prescriptions.

Thanks,

Cami / Jenni
Sent from my iPhone

▬

On Nov 29, 2016, at 10:51 AM,
R L wrote:

> I'm sure as long as he has a Dr.'s prescription, DPO B would be ok with it. She is in the office today, but is the "Officer of the Day". She is usually busy before noon. I will forward message. Hope he feels better soon.

R L
Deputy Probation Officer
Los Angeles County Probation Department

▬

From: Jenni Alpert
Date: November 29, 2016 at 12:53:06 PM PST To: R L
Subject: Re: question and update

> He now has a full medical check up appointment that I will attend tomorrow at 9am. This check up will included a lung examination to see about his upper respiratory system needs. I will email over any prescriptions to make sure they are approve before I fill them tomorrow afternoon. Below is the phone number address and Dr we will be seeing if you / Officer B have any questions.

Thanks so much
Cami / Jenni

Long Beach Comprehensive Health Center Dr. OC
Rm / 9:15am

▬

Hi Officer L,

> Hope your holidays were wonderful. Sending over an update on Don of the last several weeks to also forward on to Officer B. Although he sees her next week, he has been fighting quite a chest cold that is deeply affecting his lungs. I would like to take him to a Dr. tomorrow to see why he isn't healing on his own with the organic help I was assisting him with - perhaps there is an infection where antibiotics may be necessary. I am aware of some of the medicines he is not allowed to take at this time, so we have refrained from any and all but with a Dr.s help regarding testing to see about possible infection in his lungs I was wondering the perimeters of what he is allowed to take for help so he can end the illness and breath better.

Many thanks,

176

Cami / Jenni
Don's Daughter

From: Jenni Alpert
Date: October 28, 2016 at 1:52:49 PM PDT To: R L
Subject: Re: Don Logsdon meeting with Cornerstone Homeless Continuum / J V (Client Services) 10.27.16

Hi Officer L,
We are now leaving Hope of the Valley as there was some sort of speaker at lunch that created a longer amount of wait time than expected.
It's just about time for our newly found shared interest of drinking 3 espresso shots so I will be making a stop for Don to purchase this drink and then we will be on our way to meet with you and Officer B -

Thanks
Cami / (Jenni)

███

On Oct 28, 2016, at 9:08 AM,
R L wrote:

Please given me a call when you get a chance. R L

Deputy Probation Officer
Los Angeles County Probation Department

From: Jenni Alpert
Sent: Thursday, October 27, 2016 3:37 PM Cc: R L
Subject: Don Logsdon meeting with Cornerstone Homeless Continuum / J V (Client Services) 10.27.16

Hi J,
Thank you so much for spending time with Don Logsdon and I today at Cornerstone to brief us on the services you offer and the nature of your relationship to AB109. Upon Don's exploration of options out there for his recovery as well as his court ordered obligations we appreciate your time and efforts to inform us of all the on site day program and resources available as well as any our sources options including health care and housing that may possibility apply to Don's court order or perhaps for the future upon completing his obligations. I look forward to your email / letter with an overview of the meeting we had as well as an evaluation or any suggestion you may have for Don.

Many thanks
Don's biological Daughter (Cami / Cameron)
Jenni

███

Date: October 28, 2016 at 10:45:04 AM PDT To: R L
Subject: Re: Don Logsdon meeting with Cornerstone Homeless Continuum / J V (Client Services) 10.27.16

Hi Officer L,
We have arrived at Hope of the Valley and the AA meeting for Don's lunch and shower.
I will keep you posted of our time frame for you and Officer B.

Thank you
Cami / (Jenni)

From: Jenni Alpert
Date: October 24, 2016 at 9:01:31 PM PDT To: R L
Subject: Beit Tshuvah reference Hi Officer L,

In regards to Don Logsdon, I wanted to forward you the reference letter from Beit Tshuvah recovery home in hopes that maybe it can also be forwarded to Don's probation officer in that we can set up some sort of meeting or phone call at her earliest convenience in order to begin the process of figuring out a great place for Don to attend a recovery and sober living home of her well as the court's approval that is a good fit for his success. This
Wednesday Don has two meetings with two new options that may be a closer fit to his needs and focus and I want to double check and make sure that they are AB109 worthy as well as honorable in the courts eyes for Don's obligations.

Although he is aware of his next meeting with Officer B on November 10, it would be a great privilege for him to be placed on the waiting list of approved places before then if possible. In the meantime, upon your force having a moment to assist us with this process we will continue in the interview and research process on our own in order to present them to your office and to the court until we hear further notice of either the cast interview possibilities or approval from what we will present.

Many thanks
Cami / Jenni
Don Logsdon's Daughter

From: J M
Date: October 24, 2016 at 1:09:22 PM PDT To: Jenni Alpert
Subject: RE: Thank you for your call, re: recommendation

178

Please see the attached letter J M
Alternative Sentencing Associate
Beit T'Shuvah Residential Treatment Center

From: Jenni Alpert
Sent: Friday, October 21, 2016 6:10 PM

To: J M
Subject: Re: Thank you for your call, re: recommendation

The letter will not only be helpful, it will actually be necessary to have in order to
have in writing proof that he in fact went through the interview process and it was
that your program requests that he attend another place as a better fit for reasons
that you may also include. This in writing will help with the paper trail that shows
Don's efforts, willingness to get help, and the fact that he did show up in hopes to get
accepted. I have to get in contact with his Probation Officer to gain approval of your
recommendation should that be a fit as well as the other place he interviewed with
yesterday to make sure the Judge and his Probation Officer will in fact approve and
accept another recommendation that we for a fact also know will be a fit for Don to
assure the maximum amount of success focusing on recovery, rehabilitation, housing,
the proper emotional and mental wellnesses support and living environment that

matches his scope with Don's AB109. Calls have been put forth and interviews will continue until we hear back.

I appreciate all your time and efforts on this. Looking forward to the letter.

Many thanks
Jenni (Cami)

On Oct 21, 2016, at 2:52 PM,
J M wrote:

> Hi Jenni,
> The name of the program is HealthRight 360. It would likely be a better fit than Beit T'Shuvah for your dad. I'll email you the letter on Monday - hope it's helpful. Please say hello to Don for me, & tell him it was a pleasure to meet him. I'm sure I'll see both of you at Shabbos sometime in the near future.

Take care, J M
Alternative Sentencing Associate
Beit T'Shuvah Residential Treatment Center

From: Jenni Alpert
Sent: Friday, October 21, 2016 8:20 AM To: J
Cc: Rabbi
Subject: Thank you for your call, re: recommendation Hi J,

> Thanks so much for you call yesterday, willingness to email over a letter of interview completion for Don to show the judge, and for the recommendation Rabbi M mentioned. When you get the chance for the latter, would you be willing to remind me of the name of the place so I can research it while waiting for the letter for his case files? Don took the news very well, understood, and is ok. He had an interview with one option yesterday and we are very grateful for Rabbi suggestion as well.

Many thanks, I look forward to your email.
Jenni (Cami)

Date: October 12, 2016 at 10:06:43 AM PDT To: r.l@probation..gov
Subject: Also, heads up re: Don and his reading glasses

> Together Don and I have come to discover that Don is in fact far sighted and uses at the moment over the counter reading glasses in order to see fine print when filling out paperwork until he can make an appointment with an eye doctor to get the proper

prescription. In his focus to be on time this morning however, he left them in the car. He may need extra help from his probation officer with reading but may not express this.

Thanks
Jenni (Cami)

████

From: Jenni Alpert
Date: October 12, 2016 at 9:01:33 AM PDT To: R L R.L@probation.lacounty.gov>
Subject: Re: Update: Don Logsdon / Kol Nidre q Hi Officer L

Don is currently on the blue line metro from the Washington stop traveling towards Long Beach now to meet his probation officer at 10am. He plans to check in and register as a drug addict just before hand across the street per your request.

Thank you
Jenni (Cami)

████

On Oct 11, 2016, at 11:26 AM,
R L wrote:

Hello Ms. Alpert,
I am very pleased to see all of the pictures of your dad with a smile on his face and looking well. I will find out today who your father was assigned to and forward this message. I am truly happy to see those pictures of him doing well.

R L
Deputy Probation Officer
Los Angeles County Probation Department

████

From: Jenni Alpert
Sent: Saturday, October 08, 2016 2:08 PM To: R L
Subject: Fwd: Update: Don Logsdon / Kol Nidre q Hi Officer L,

This is Jenni Alpert, otherwise named Cameron Morantz before adoption, Don Logsdon's biological daughter. I met you the other day at the end of Don's meeting with you for his next meeting this coming Wed at 10am to meet with his assigned probation officer as obtain information of his responsibilities for the next phase of his life.

Thank you for taking your time to meet with me and for giving me your card. I wanted to forward you my correspondence and updates with Recovery Home: Beit T'shuvah so that you and Don's soon to be probation officer can be abreast of his progress and willingness to learn the tools and possibilities of opportunity for another way of life of any kind should he feel interest and ready. With my assistance and his own will he has been attending different Jewish events to learn more about part of his heritage as a preparation should he be accepted into Beit T'shuvah, a

Jewish based recovery home. If not for any reason we will need other options to apply for that will fit into his needs as soon as possible. In addition he is attending AA meetings with my assistance to see a different perspective of why attending them can help him be of service for others himself.

Next Wed is Yom Kippur the end to the Jewish New Year and I not be able to attend with Don for his meeting but I see this as a good opportunity for him to choose self reliance should he. However, I would like to keep in touch and continue to assist as I can. He needs to be in a safe environment away from gangs, drug pushers, and violence so any suggestion you may have for low to no income probationers please let me know,

Thank you,
Jenni (Cami)
Sent from my iPhone

▬

From: Jenni Alpert
Date: October 8, 2016 at 1:59:24 PM PDT To: C N
Cc: r@beittshuvah.org
Subject: Update: Don Logsdon / Kol Nidre q

Hi C and Rabbi, per request, I am sending another update on Don Logsdon for possible review for entry in the recovery program.

Since Don has been released from Jail on Wed Oct 5th after turning himself in to begin taking control of his probation responsibilities, he has been taking steps towards his own education on obtaining tools for recovery and options out there with my assistance. It appears that he has his own motivation and interest and upon seeing options and learning of social services to help people who have been in Jail or Prison dealing with drug and other addictions, crime, the need for mental health awareness, and safe affordable housing challenges as well as the value of a recovery home. Pictures below are his willingness to attend AA meetings and view them from a new perspective expressing future interest to offer help to those in need themselves, visiting the self realization center to see a different view of God, and attended Shabbat services with me choosing on his own to pay respect for the temple wearing a Kippah and Tallis.

On his own accord he asked to visit the officer of the day early to get information of what will be expected of him in terms of his probation responsibilities and they have assigned him a meeting this coming Wed to meet his new probation officer. Today he asked if anyone would ever hire him to do a job where he could earn money to eventually obtain safe low income housing away from large groups of people as he didn't think he could ever get hired to do something he is good at (teach, music, carpentry) as an ex convict.

I am aware that M visited him while he was in jail and asked him to call on his release date while awaiting evaluation.

During this busy period of the High Holidays as Don learns more of the traditions of the Jews, understands that there will be a window of time where he is to maintain his own discipline, however as for a recovery home, he has expressed interest in yours as a first choice should he still be up for consideration.

182

In the meantime, I was wondering what it may take for him and I and my partner to attend Kol Nidre services together with your congregation so he can get more of a feel for Rabbi M. If it is possible please let me know and I look forward to speaking with you soon.

Thanks so much, Shana Tovah
Jenni Alpert

On Aug 2, 2016, at 10:41 AM, C wrote:

Hi Jenni,
Why don't you give me a call when you have a chance, or send me your number and I will call you, so I can get a little bit of the "backstory" about your birth father. I'm a little unclear regarding his situation, but would like to be able to help, if possible.

Alternative Sentencing Coordinator

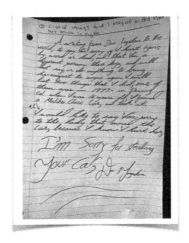

In the event that anything should ever happen to me, the travel trailer is willed to Don Logsdon if he wants, wherever he may wish to stay and I will let you know my delegated point person to follow his wishes and look after his well being. Option A: Location of safety lodging - S RV Park Scotia CA Contact: (B) see below!

Thanks,
Cami / Jenni

This is Cami, daughter and advocate for Don Logsdon. Feel free to email me the case manager permission form here!

Thanks
Cami aka Jenni Alpert

Quotes
Jenni Alpert

"If you can help one person you help the world."

"It's not that my birth father was homeless having nothing lost in the world exactly - by his words he would say it was the freedom he always wanted that he never had - out there on his own living it his way.

What is so wrong with that really? When you don't need anything from the world, it's right there ready to give you everything."

"It's never to late to be who we are present as we evolve to become the continuing of shedding layers of what we were meant to be in yesterday's tomorrows now"

"You never notice the value of time until you start to sense your running out of it "

"When you can be wide open and curious to be part of someone else's world, in this the home where I fit best."

"Take a risk and love your heart out"

ABOUT THE AUTHOR

Jenni Alpert (Cami) - Singer, songwriter, guitarist, and pianist Jenni Alpert (Birth name: Cameron, Cami) was born in Los Angeles, CA and adopted out of the foster care system at the age of four. She started to sing and play piano while staying in various foster homes. With the encouragement and support of her adoptive family, she learned to play the guitar as well and began writing and record songs early. With her honest rich songwriting and soothing musical melodies, songstress Jenni Alpert's haunting, powerful, and sultry voice has gained the respect of fans and music tastemakers worldwide. Her emotionally driven songs weave a unique web of eclectic Soul-Americana Pop. As familiar with jazz and Americana as she is pop, Alpert graduated from UCLA in the Ethnomusicology Department after completing a four-year jazz program headed by Kenny Burrell. No stranger to the recording studio, Alpert has released 8 albums and has independently toured over 14 countries with regularity. Upon reuniting with her biological father who was homeless, addicted, and running from the law at the time, yet a musician just like her, a film team decided to make a short documentary entitled *Homeless: the Soundtrack* directed by Oscar-nominated, Peabody and Emmy Award winning documentary film director Irene Taylor Brodsky, produced by Steve and Paula Mae Schwartz about the early stages that unfold the journey of their biological reunion capturing the unique bond they share. The two currently perform and share their biological reunion adventures and on creative approaches towards transformation in story and song together alongside supporting the film as a duo under the name *Cami and Don, The Biological Duo.*

Don Logsdon - the biological father of singer songwriter Jenni Alpert aka birth name Cami used to be addicted and running from the law while straddling incarceration and homelessness but also unbeknownst to them alike, was a musician just like his daughter. Upon their reunion shy of four years ago while discovering their mutuality in music and attachment, he chose to change his life and try new things introduced to him by his daughter to develop a deeper relationship with her. As their music kinship and personal relationship solidified, together the two embarked upon a unique reunion journey that now has lead them to performing music together as 'Cami and Don the Biological Duo' for various organizations: Hope of the Valley Rescue Mission Van Nuys Help Center for the Homeless, Celia Center, Inc. for the adopted and fostered, and Concerned United Birthparents, to name a few - performing, speaking, and sharing stories about their biological reunion, transformation, and the impacts foster care, adoption, homelessness, addiction, incarceration, and support or the lack thereof have on any individual connected to these topics offering ideas on how to uniquely solution solve to overcome or work with them. He is also the other subject with his daughter in the up and coming short documentary *Homeless: The Soundtrack* directed by Irene Taylor Brodsky produced by Chockstone Pictures about the early stages of their reunion and their miraculous biological journey to transformation.